The Quotable Saint Jerome

The
Quotable
Saint Jerome

Justin McClain, Editor

FOREWORD BY SCOTT HAHN

The Catholic University of America Press

Washington, D.C.

The paper used in this publication meets the minimum requirements of American

National Standards for Information Science—Permanence of Paper for Printed Library

Materials, ANSI Z39.48-1984.

∞

Cataloging-in-Publication data available from the Library of Congress.

ISBN: 978-0-8132-3321-5.

Contents

Doctrine   34

Eternity   38

The Incarnation 66

Judgment 72

Sin 147

Suffering and the Cross 152

The Trinity 155

Wisdom 161

Editor's Note

The year 2020 marks sixteen hundred years since the death of Saint Jerome, priest and Doctor of the Church. Saint Jerome's contributions to the Church can hardly be overestimated. From his translation of the Sacred Scriptures from their original Hebrew (Old Testament) and Greek (a few parts of the Old Testament and the entirety of the New Testament), we have the fruits of that holy labor in what is popularly deemed the *Vulgate Bible*. The Catholic Church relied upon the *Vulgate* for approximately one thousand years, and it is still frequently referenced in the modern era.

In Jerome's early life, he did not care as much about theological matters until he experienced a renewal of faith as a young adult. In addition to Jerome's renown as a biblical scholar, he was foremost a faithful priest, a patient spiritual director, a humble hermit in the tradition of Saint Anthony the Abbot (the "father of desert monasticism"), an ardent foe of heresy, and a zealous catechist, along with performing various other vital ministerial roles. In the pages of this text, which, for the first time in English, contain Saint Jerome's sayings specifically organized by topic, you will come to know more about what Saint Jerome had to say on a myriad of points within Catholicism. May the knowledge that you gain, a product of the sharp wit and severe humility of this remarkable man, lead you to a devotion to this holy figure. Likewise, may his sanctifying example and prayerful intercession lead you all the more to a deeper relationship with the Lord Jesus Christ, whom Jerome adored with the fullness of his time and energy, through the end of his earthly life, for which he gained the eternal "crown of life" (James 1:2; Revelation 2:10).

Acknowledgments

This text is dedicated to the community of The Catholic University of America, and in a special way to the staff of CUA Press. Catholic University brought my wife Bernadette ('07) to the DC area, so if not for her having studied there, we likely never would have met. Thank you to acquisitions editor John Martino, editorial director Dr. Trevor Lipscombe, and all of their peers at CUA Press for their patience and support in the year plus that it took me to complete this project.

— Mr. Justin McClain, OP, January 17, 2020
(Memorial of Saint Anthony the Abbot)

Publisher's Note

The quotations in this book come from the works of Jerome published by The Catholic University of America Press and are presented here in their original form, except in certain cases when punctuation and capitalization have been slightly altered so that the quote can appear seamlessly on the page. Items in square brackets [ ] are interpolations found in the original translation; items in braces { } are interpolations for the purposes of this book. Some introductory clauses are omitted, such as "for this reason," if the prior idea is not relevant to the quotation. The footnotes from the original translation are reproduced in some cases in this text using parenthetical citations, but not every footnote has been included so as to not burden the reader.

The title of the work in question is given in the parenthetical citation; sometimes the title corresponds to the title of the published English translation, such as the *Commentary on Matthew*, and sometimes it is a work included within a published book, such as *The Dialogue Against the Pelagians*, which appears inside the published book *Dogmatic and Polemical Works*. In all cases, the volume number of the FOTC (Fathers of the Church series) will point to the appropriate English version.

One of the works of Jerome cited for this book is his *Commentary on Galatians*. A significant topic in Paul's letter to the Galatians is the transition from the 'Old Law' of Israel to the 'New Law' of Jesus. Following Paul, Jerome engages in sustained polemics against an interpretation of Christianity that would require the following of the Mosaic law. This exaltation of Christ may seem at times a denigration of Judaism, and some passages of that text may not be considered congenial to the modern ear cognizant of the danger of Christian anti-Semitism. These passages, especially if taken out of context, are some of the 'less quotable Saint Jerome' and are not included here; the reader will find some passages that speak of the Old Law and the

New, but the present book does not dwell on these comparisons as much as Jerome himself did in that particular commentary. It does not shy away from Jerome's (and Paul's) central teaching about the excellence and pre-eminence of the New Law. It should also be noted that Jerome also defended the Old Law "against the heretics, especially Marcion, Valentinus, and everyone else who undermines the Old Testament…whatever excuse they give for Paul, we shall return in kind with a defense of the Old Law" (*Commentary on Galatians*, Book Three (Galatians 5.7–6.18), 5.12 (FOTC 121)).

Foreword

Celebrities—in every time and place—run the risk of imprisonment in their personae. No matter what they accomplish, no matter what they do, people already know how to frame the story. Their friends may accentuate the positive, their enemies the negative. But friend and foe alike will highlight the personality traits that are distinctive, the particular prodigies and the eccentricities.

Alas for Jerome of Stridon, whose prodigies were great, but whose eccentricities were prodigiously entertaining.

The poet Phyllis McGinley caricatured him as "the great name-caller." And he could trade insults with the best, deriding an erstwhile companion as an "effeminate soldier" for leaving behind the rigors of monastic life. He could be touchy and critical. He quarreled with many, including Augustine. He was dismissive of the accomplishments of Ambrose and Chrysostom.

When he is remembered at all, it seems, he is remembered for these idiosyncrasies. Preachers invoke him in order to give hope to their congregations: "If even Jerome could achieve sainthood, then so can you!"

It is undeniable that Jerome had what his biographer, J. N. D. Kelly, called "a complex, curiously ambivalent personality." I fear, however, that we too often reduce him to the caricature. We speak of him as that odd saint, but we speak only about his oddities while ignoring his sanctity.

This is a gross injustice. Jerome was, after all, the man who produced a readable vernacular translation of the Bible for the West—one that Christians from Carthage to Eboracum could love. His Latin Vulgate remained the bedrock of western civilization for more than a millennium. Our laws and literature echo his phrasing.

Jerome was also a pioneer in the fields of patristics and patrology. The biographies he wrote in *Illustrious Men*, with their bibliographical data, are the starting point for our study of many great figures of antiquity. Most of his entries are brief, comprised of only the titles of major works; but Jerome's passing reference is sometimes the only evidence we have of texts that are otherwise lost and forgotten. Some figures, however, receive fulsome biographies, and it is interesting to see who they are: Irenaeus of Lyons, Clement of Alexandria, (curiously) Philo of Alexandria—and Origen, whom Jerome later turned upon with a vengeance.

Jerome was also a great catalyst in the development of religious life for women. Almost alone among his contemporaries, he recognized females as his equals (or betters) in scholarship, churchmanship, and asceticism. He promoted the work of Paula, Eustochium, Marcella, Fabiola, Melania. They, in turn, established monastic communities, conducted scholarly research, and helped to invent the hospital.

In all of history, moreover, Jerome stands out as the great promoter of pilgrimage. As a young man he wandered the dark, unmarked, fetid corridors of the Roman Catacombs. He relished the nearness of his Christian forebears. He learned from the inscriptions on the walls and the graffiti scratched in plaster. Later in life, Jerome moved to the Holy Land and wrote letters that have served ever since as tourist-promotion brochures.

As well they should. No matter what the subject, Jerome always wrote memorably and quotably. Yes, he swore off Cicero; but only after he had completely absorbed and mastered his art of epigram.

I live more than a millennium and a half after the death of Jerome, and yet I find myself repeating one of his lines at least once a week: "Ignorance of Scripture is ignorance of Christ." Nobody before or since has said it better. Cicero never gave the world anything quoted quite so often or with so much relish.

Jerome was a controversialist. He could not remain silent in the face of heresy or bad behavior. He brought the full Ciceronian force of his rhetoric to bear in the great arguments of his time. A number of his works begin with the word "Against"—*Against Helvidius, Against Jovinianus, Against Vigilantius, Against the Pelagians, Against Rufinus.*

And this certainly colors our modern-day perceptions of the man. He did not suffer fools; nor would he fail to point out his opponents' foolishness for the sake of diplomacy. To his great credit, he was effective. The errors of Helvidius and Vigilantius went down hard, and they did not stagger to their feet again until the sixteenth century.

It is easy to see why so much of Jerome's great work is forgotten. He translated the Bible into a language that is no longer anyone's vernacular. His biblical commentaries were foundational studies in a science that is cumulative; what he wrote was designed to be surpassed in future generations.

Other works, however, deserve to be remembered and are not. His letters of spiritual direction are masterpieces of the art. They are addressed to individual men and individual women. They are eminently practical. They are psychologically astute. They are deeply biblical. They are realist in every way. His letter to Nepotian stands as a fairly complete program of priestly formation that priests and seminarians today would do well to read in its entirety once a year.

Jerome was a sage. He was a man of prayer. He was a sensitive pastor and doctor of souls. He was funny, sometimes, in endearing ways. He was strangely humble, and he knew himself.

As I prepared to write this foreword, I jotted down my favorite quotes from Justin McClain's manuscript, but I soon found I was simply reproducing the book. Very few of my favorites conform to the popular notion of Jerome as a crotchety man, elderly from his youth.

Every caricature contains an element of truth, which it emphasizes to unreal proportions. Every caricature is thus untrue and, to some extent, unjust. Our caricatures of Jerome can be useful insofar as they give us hope for attaining sanctity.

If we truly want to pursue sanctity, however, after the fashion of Jerome, we need to encounter him as a man in full, a man with heroic virtues and achievements, a man in love with Jesus Christ.

We need to move on from entertainment to edification, and now we can do so by the shortest course—in the pages of this book.

Angels

1. We shall not be angels, but like angels. Do not let that seem a slight thing to you, O man, if you shall be like an angel.
Homilies on the Psalms, Homily 21, Psalm 91 (92) (FOTC 48)

2. Every last one of us is in need of God's compassion. Gabriel, Michael, Seraphim, Cherubim, Powers, Dominations, all are holy, indeed, but stand in need just the same of the mercy of their Creator. I am not detracting from the angels, but I am proclaiming their Creator, inasmuch as the angels have themselves given Him glory, freely and gladly.
Homilies on the Psalms, Homily 34, Psalm 107 (108) (FOTC 48)

3. The children of God, all the just, are borne upon the hands of angels—for protection—at the Lord's injunction.
Homilies on the Psalms: Second Series, Homily 68, Psalm 90 (91) (FOTC 57)

4. The Lord too can fulfill what he wants, not so much by coming in person, as by the ministries of angels.
Commentary on Matthew, Book One (Matthew 1.1–10.42), 8.9 (FOTC 117)

5. The worth of souls is so great that from birth each one has an angel assigned to him for his protection.
Commentary on Matthew, Book Three (Matthew 16.13–22.40), 18.10 (FOTC 117)

6. Even as among men there are various orders, distinguished by the work itself, since the bishop, priest, and every ecclesiastical order have their own rank, and they, nevertheless, all remain human beings; so also among angels there are different merits, and they all, nevertheless,

retain their angelic dignity. Men are not created from angels, nor are men changed back again into angels.
The Apology Against the Books of Rufinus, Book One, paragraph 23 (FOTC 53)

The Beatitudes, Happiness, and Joy

7. If, however, I do not remain in the state of sin, but withdraw from sin, I become happy once more.
Homilies on the Psalms, Homily 1, Psalm 1 (FOTC 48)

8. Just as he who has not stood—persisted—in sin is happy, so he who has not sat—persisted—in evil doctrine is happy.
Homilies on the Psalms, Homily 1, Psalm 1 (FOTC 48)

9. You see yourselves that the three determinants of beatitude consist in not thinking evil, in not persevering in sin, and in not teaching evil.
Homilies on the Psalms, Homily 1, Psalm 1 (FOTC 48)

10. The Old Law lays down, as it were, only one condition of blessedness; the Gospel, on the other hand, announces simultaneously eight beatitudes.
Homilies on the Psalms, Homily 1, Psalm 1 (FOTC 48)

11. Whoever love the name of the Lord, they will rejoice.
Homilies on the Psalms, Homily 2, Psalm 5 (FOTC 48)

12. To see God is an infinite crown.
Homilies on the Psalms, Homily 16, Psalm 83 (84) (FOTC 48)

13. The face of God makes the just shine with joy.
Homilies on the Psalms, Homily 30, Psalm 103 (104) (FOTC 48)

14. What happiness, after all, is there in the things of the world that can compare with the happiness of heaven?
Homilies on the Psalms, Homily 41, Psalm 119 (120) (FOTC 48)

15. The advent of Christ has reference to the maturation of the human race.
Commentary on Galatians, Book Two (Galatians 3.10–5.6), 4.1–2 (FOTC 121)

The Blessed Virgin Mary

THE BLESSED VIRGIN MARY—*Intercession*

16. [Mary] leads us back to heaven.
Homilies on the Psalms: Second Series, Homily 73, Psalm 96 (97) (FOTC 57)

THE BLESSED VIRGIN MARY—*The Nativity*

17. Behold Truth, the Savior, is born of earth, that is, of Mary.
Homilies on the Psalms, Homily 17, Psalm 84 (85) (FOTC 48)

18. [Mary] was a holy woman, had read the Sacred Scriptures, knew the prophets, and was recalling that the angel Gabriel had said to her the same things that the prophets had foretold.
Various Homilies, Homily 88—On the Nativity of the Lord (FOTC 57)

THE BLESSED VIRGIN MARY—*Perpetual Virginity*

19. Holy Mary [it is] with child of no human seed.
Homilies on the Psalms, Homily 24, Psalm 96 (97) (FOTC 48)

20. Holy Mary, blessed Mary, mother and virgin, virgin before giving birth, virgin after giving birth! I, for my part, marvel how a virgin is born of a virgin, and how, after the birth of a virgin, the mother is a virgin. ... Attribute to the power of God, then, that He was born of a virgin, and the virgin herself after bringing forth was a virgin still.
Various Homilies, Homily 87—On the Gospel of John 1.1–14 (FOTC 57)

21. Certain people most perversely surmise that Mary also had other sons. They claim that there could not be talk of a firstborn unless there are brothers, although it is the custom of the Holy Scriptures to call "firstborn" not one who is followed by brothers, but the first to be born.
Commentary on Matthew, Book One (Matthew 1.1–10.42), 1.24–25 (FOTC 117)

22. Some surmise that the brothers of the Lord are sons of Joseph by another wife. They follow apocryphal nonsense, fabricating some little woman named Escha. But as the book that we have written against Helvidius shows, we understand the brothers of the Lord to be not sons of Joseph, but first cousins of the Savior. They are children of the Mary who was the Lord's aunt, who is said to be the mother of James the less and of Joses and Jude. We read in another passage of the Gospel that they are called brothers of the Lord. Now all of Scripture demonstrates that first cousins are called brothers.
Commentary on Matthew, Book Two (Matthew 11.2–16.12), 12.49 (FOTC 117)

23. The new tomb can also point to the virginal womb of Mary.
Commentary on Matthew, Book Four (Matthew 22.41–28.20), 27.60 (FOTC 117)

24. We must invoke the Holy Spirit to defend through our lips and his understanding the virginity of the Blessed Mary.
On the Perpetual Virginity of the Blessed Mary Against Helvidius, paragraph 2 (FOTC 53)

25. If anybody has feelings of scruples because a virgin conceived when she was betrothed rather than without a betrothed, or (as Scripture calls him) a husband, let him know it was done for three reasons: first, that the origin of Mary might also be revealed through the lineage of Joseph, to whom she was related; second, that she might not be stoned as an adulteress according to the law of Moses; third, that, in her flight to Egypt, she might have the solacing comfort of a guardian rather than of a husband.
On the Perpetual Virginity of the Blessed Mary Against Helvidius, paragraph 4 (FOTC 53)

26. Elizabeth and Zacharia can teach us… of the womb, how vastly inferior they are, as regards sanctity, to the blessed Mary, the mother of God, who, [is] conscious that God was dwelling within her…
The Dialogue Against the Pelagians, Book One, paragraph 16 (FOTC 53)

The Catholic Church

THE CATHOLIC CHURCH—*Apostolic Succession*

27. Whom can we name as foundations? The apostles. Upon them the foundations were laid; where the faith of the Church was first established, there, too, the foundations were laid.
Homilies on the Psalms, Homily 18, Psalm 86 (87) (FOTC 48)

28. With the exception of the apostles, whatever else is said afterwards should be removed and not, later on, hold the force of authority. No matter how holy anyone may be after the time of the apostles, no matter how eloquent, he does not have authority, for "in his record of the peoples and princes the Lord shall tell of those who have been born in her" (Psalm 87.6).
Homilies on the Psalms, Homily 18, Psalm 86 (87) (FOTC 48)

29. By this way—through the Lord and Savior—they might enter the city of their home, might enter his Church that He had built upon himself, the Rock, the Way, the Guide.
Homilies on the Psalms, Homily 33, Psalm 106 (107) (FOTC 48)

30. We are of the Church if we believe the truth of Christian teaching, acknowledge Christ. ... If, as I was saying, we are in the Church, if we possess the faith of the Church, of the apostles, of Christ, the truths of Christian teaching, we are the mountains of Sion.
Homilies on the Psalms, Homily 45, Psalm 132 (133) (FOTC 48)

31. The prophets in truth are the gates of the Church; we cannot enter the Church except through them. Manichaeus tried to enter without the gates and could not. Marcion rejects the Old Testament, but without it, he has not been able to enter the New. We, on the other hand, accept the prophet-gates, and through them, make our entrance.
Homilies on the Psalms, Homily 57, Psalm 147 (147B) (FOTC 48)

32. Peter is chosen upon whom the Church is to be built, and James, the first of the apostles who is to be crowned with martyrdom, and John, who initiates the state of virginity.
Homilies on the Gospel of Saint Mark on Various Topics, Homily 77 (III)—On Mark 5.30–43 (FOTC 57)

33. He is speaking to the apostles, and upon them He has established the Church, whatever He says to them, He is saying to the Church, for it has only one body, but many members. ... The Church has real eyes: manifestly its churchmen and teachers who see in Holy Writ the mysteries of God, and to them applies the Scriptural appellation of "seer" (1 Kings 9.9). It is correct, then, to call these seers the eyes of the Church. It also has hands, effective men who, of course, are not eyes, but hands. Do they know the mysteries of Holy Writ? No, but they are powerful in works. The Church has feet. Those who are feet are not those who see, nor those who work, but those who make

official journeys of all kinds; the foot runs that the hand may find the work that it is to do. The eye does not scorn the hand, nor does the hand scorn the foot, nor do these three scorn the belly as if it were idle and unemployed.
Various Homilies, Homily 85—On the Gospel of Matthew 18.7–9 (FOTC 57)

34. Upon this rock the Lord founded the Church; from this rock also the Apostle Peter was allotted his name.
Commentary on Matthew, Book One (Matthew 1.1–10.42), 7.25 (FOTC 117)

35. Christ is the Bridegroom, the Church is the bride. From this holy and spiritual marriage, the Apostles were created.
Commentary on Matthew, Book One (Matthew 1.1–10.42), 9.15 (FOTC 117)

36. Jesus, through the figure of the Apostles and the boat, leads the Church across to the shore, a Church delivered from the shipwreck of persecutions, and … he has it find rest in a most tranquil harbor.
Commentary on Matthew, Book Two (Matthew 11.2–16.12), 14.34 (FOTC 117)

THE CATHOLIC CHURCH—*Doctrine*

37. The Church does not consist in walls, but in the truths of her teachings. The Church is there where there is true faith.
Homilies on the Psalms, Homily 46, Psalm 133 (134) (FOTC 48)

38. [The Lord Jesus'] kindness He preserves perpetually in the Church which He has redeemed through the covenant of his commandments.
Homilies on the Psalms: Second Series, Homily 66, Psalm 88 (89) (FOTC 57)

39. Let Celsus, then, learn, and Porphyry and Julian, those rabid dogs barking against Christ; let their followers learn—those who think that the church has had no philosophers, no orators, no men of learning; let them learn the number and quality of the men who founded, built, and adorned the church and let them stop accusing our faith of such rustic simplicity, and recognize instead their own ignorance.
On Illustrious Men, Preface, paragraph 7 (FOTC 100)

40. When you confess that I am Catholic in every respect, you will not be able to impute to me the charge of heresy.
The Apology Against the Books of Rufinus, Book Three, paragraph 27 (FOTC 53)

41. I have never spared heretics, and have endeavored in every possible manner to make the enemies of the Church my own enemies.
The Dialogue Against the Pelagians, Preface, paragraph 2 (FOTC 53)

42. It is the hope and prayer of all of us who profess the Catholic faith that heresy be refuted and individuals be converted. Or, if they choose to persist in error, the blame is certainly not to be placed on us…, but rather on those who have preferred falsehood to truth.
The Dialogue Against the Pelagians, Preface, paragraph 2 (FOTC 53)

43. He kills a heretic who allows him to be a heretic. However, our reproving gives you life, so that being dead to heresy, you may live for the Catholic faith.
The Dialogue Against the Pelagians, Book Three, paragraph 17 (FOTC 53)

THE CATHOLIC CHURCH—*God's Sovereignty*

44. The Church is [God's] house; also [his] temple.
Homilies on the Psalms, Homily 2, Psalm 5 (FOTC 48)

45. Behold you are the Church that has been assembled in the name of God; for this reason do we say, may God have pity on us and bless us.
Homilies on the Psalms, Homily 6, Psalm 66 (67) (FOTC 48)

46. The faith of the Church is not laid in the valleys, but is established on the mountains.
Homilies on the Psalms, Homily 18, Psalm 86 (87) (FOTC 48)

47. The Lord is King, and He is robed in the splendor of patriarchs and prophets and a people that believes. He is robed in splendor: the patriarchs and prophets have been as the garment of Christ.
Homilies on the Psalms, Homily 26, Psalm 98 (99) (FOTC 48)

48. Wherever there is the vision of peace, wherever there is contemplation of God, there should also be the praise of God. Therefore, O Church, glorify the Lord; because you have begun to believe in Him and to possess peace, you have also begun to see peace, Jerusalem, the vision of peace. You, who were formerly the slave of idols, have become the servant of God; therefore, glorify your God. ... O ecclesiastical soul, you, O Church.
Homilies on the Psalms, Homily 57, Psalm 147 (147B) (FOTC 48)

49. Children of the Church, children of a new people, let them rejoice in their king, in Christ, who reigns over them.
Homilies on the Psalms, Homily 59, Psalm 149 (FOTC 48)

50. Jesus the High Priest ... lays the foundations of the Church and erects the spiritual Jerusalem.
Homilies on the Psalms: Second Series, Homily 61, Psalm 15 (16) (FOTC 57)

51. Although the Church shines as the moon in the nighttime, nevertheless, we cannot dwell in the full splendor of the true Sun.
Various Homilies, Homily 91—On the Exodus (*The Vigil of Easter*) (FOTC 57)

52. The church, however, is barren without her husband Christ.
Commentary on Galatians, Book Two (Galatians 3.10–5.6), 4.27 (FOTC 121)

THE CATHOLIC CHURCH—*Membership*

53. They, indeed, who have been baptized in the Church call the Church "Mother."
Homilies on the Psalms, Homily 18, Psalm 86 (87) (FOTC 48)

54. All who dwell in [the Church] are, as it were, full of joy and gladness.
Homilies on the Psalms, Homily 18, Psalm 86 (87) (FOTC 48)

55. Let us interpret the moon in another way as the Church; for in propagating the Church, we increase with her; when she suffers persecution and is decreased, we suffer persecution and decrease with her.
Homilies on the Psalms, Homily 30, Psalm 103 (104) (FOTC 48)

56. The whole Church throughout the world praises the Lord every day.
Homilies on the Psalms, Homily 35, Psalm 108 (109) (FOTC 48)

57. The Lord blesses in the Church.
Homilies on the Psalms, Homily 35, Psalm 108 (109) (FOTC 48)

58. Not in Judea alone, but in the whole world, in the Church, I will praise [the Lord].
Homilies on the Psalms, Homily 35, Psalm 108 (109) (FOTC 48)

59. Wherever there is a choir many voices blend into one song. In the same way that separate chords produce a single effect, so, too, do separate voices harmonize as one. In other words, when the faithful gather together, they form the Lord's choir. Let them praise His name in choir.
Homilies on the Psalms, Homily 59, Psalm 149 (FOTC 48)

60. The Church is the body of Christ and we are members.
Homilies on the Psalms: Second Series, Homily 61, Psalm 15 (16) (FOTC 57)

61. All {who}soever, indeed, who are in the Church, are called in common the Lord's people.
Homilies on the Psalms: Second Series, Homily 64, Psalm 84 (85) (FOTC 57)

62. It is the mystery of the Church that is being prefigured, the Church gathered together from many nations so that, from separate places and from diverse regions and customs, one choir may sound forth the praise of God.
Homilies on the Psalms: Second Series, Homily 65, Psalm 87 (88) (FOTC 57)

63. Would you like to know how the Church is built up from water and blood? First, through the baptism of water, sins are forgiven; then, the blood of martyrs crowns the edifice. … It is evident that the Church is established by the kindness of God.
Homilies on the Psalms: Second Series, Homily 66, Psalm 88 (89) (FOTC 57)

64. The truth is being revealed that no one is to be excluded from the Church without the hope of coming back, for just as divine severity terrifies with manifest justice, so even does paternal love restore with a tempering clemency.
Homilies on the Psalms: Second Series, Homily 66, Psalm 88 (89) (FOTC 57)

65. The Church, gathered together from the Gentiles, is offering the Savior her gifts, the faith of believers.
Homilies on the Gospel of Saint Mark on Various Topics, Homily 84 (X)—On Mark 13.32–3 and 14.3–6 (FOTC 57)

66. The house of God is the Church, the wonderful tabernacle, for in it abide cries of joy and thanksgiving and all the sounds of festival.
Various Homilies, Homily 92, Psalm 41 (42) (FOTC 57)

67. Faith in {the Son of man} shines in the Catholic churches from the east as far as the west. The following should also be said: that the second coming of the Savior will be manifested not in humility, as the first, but in glory. And so, it is foolish to look in a small or hidden place for him who is the light of the whole world.
Commentary on Matthew, Book Four (Matthew 22.41–28.20), 24.27 (FOTC 117)

68. The Church is made up of two parts. One has neither spot nor wrinkle and is truly the body of Christ, while the other assembles in the name of Christ but is not mature in virtue.
Commentary on Galatians, Book One (Galatians 1.1–3.9), 1.2 (FOTC 121)

69. If anyone is looking for eloquence or enjoys rhetorical declamations, he has Demosthenes and Polemon in Greek and Cicero and Quintilian in Latin. The church of Christ has drawn its members not from the Academy or the Lycaeum but from the common people.
Commentary on Galatians, Book Three (Galatians 5.7–6.18), Preface (FOTC 121)

70. The members in the one Church are different.
The Dialogue Against the Pelagians, Book One, paragraph 16 (FOTC 53)

THE CATHOLIC CHURCH—*Monasticism*

71. Philo the Jew…engaged in praise of us Christians, recalling that they existed, not just there, but in many provinces, and calling their dwellings monasteries.

From this it is apparent that the first church of believers in Christ was such as the monks now imitate and emulate, so that nothing is held in private by anyone, not one among them is rich, not one poor,

their patrimonies are divided among the needy, they spend their time in prayer and the psalms, in doctrine and continence, just as Luke describes how believers lived at the beginning in Jerusalem.
On Illustrious Men, XI. Philo the Jew, 1-2 (FOTC 100)

THE CATHOLIC CHURCH—*Sainthood*

72. The city of the Lord is the Church of the saints, the assembly of the just.
Homilies on the Psalms, Homily 27, Psalm 100 (101) (FOTC 48)

73. We may even understand the land of God to be the Church: to the saints within it, all the desires of God are seen to be wonderful; to people outside, nothing seems wonderful that is even truly marvelous by its very nature. May we be in the land of God, and may we be transformed into the image of the Savior, and may He accomplish wonderfully in us all His desires.
Homilies on the Psalms: Second Series, Homily 61, Psalm 15 (16) (FOTC 57)

74. The Lord speaks to His people, to all Christians, in fact, and to His saints who are the foremost faithful in the Church, and to those who come back to Him wholeheartedly—those who do penance.
Homilies on the Psalms: Second Series, Homily 64, Psalm 84 (85) (FOTC 57)

75. The Church will abide in the brightness of the glory that is to come.
Homilies on the Psalms: Second Series, Homily 66, Psalm 88 (89) (FOTC 57)

76. If, according to the apostle, we are the temple and the house of God, then, the holiness of our conduct ought to be an honor and ornament of the Church; if, on the contrary, sins and vices are

discovered in us, then, we are the dishonor and pollution of the house of the Lord, not its beauty.
Homilies on the Psalms: Second Series, Homily 70, Psalm 92 (93) (FOTC 57)

77. There are two gates: the gate of Paradise and the gate of the Church. Through the gate of the one, we enter the gate of the other. … Every saint enters by this gate, no matter how much the devil tries to prevent him.
Various Homilies, Homily 93—On Easter Sunday (FOTC 57)

78. The pillars of the church are the apostles, and especially Peter, James, and John, two of whom were deemed worthy to climb the mountain with the Lord. … All believers who have conquered Satan can become pillars of the church.
Commentary on Galatians, Book One (Galatians 1.1–3.9), 2.7–9 (FOTC 121)

79. Where else [but in Rome] do [Christians] so enthusiastically rush in droves to the churches and martyrs' tombs? Where else does "Amen" reverberate like thunderclaps in the sky, and where else are the empty shrines of false gods shaken to the core? The Romans' faith is no different from the faith that all of Christ's churches have, though their sense of pious devotion and the innocence of their belief are superior to all. And yet Paul rebuked them for being prideful and too easily swayed by bad influences.
Commentary on Galatians, Book Two (Galatians 3.10–5.6), Preface (FOTC 121)

THE CATHOLIC CHURCH—*Tradition*

80. The sign of the cross is our banner.
Homilies on the Psalms, Homily 19, Psalm 89 (90) (FOTC 48)

81. We are not airing our own opinion, but supporting tradition.
Various Homilies, Homily 88—On the Nativity of the Lord (FOTC 57)

Charity

Charity—*Conversion*

82. Would to heaven this solitude were granted us, that it would clear away all wickedness from our tongue, so that where there are thorns, where there are brambles, where there are nettles, the fire of the Lord may come and burn all of it and make it a desert place, the solitude of Christ.
Homilies on the Psalms, Homily 41, Psalm 119 (120) (FOTC 48)

83. May the Lord grant that no cold ever creep into our hearts. We do not commit sin except after charity has grown cold.
Homilies on the Psalms, Homily 57, Psalm 147 (147B) (FOTC 48)

84. If love is taken out of the equation, villainy prevails in society and people go on the attack and finally are consumed by one another. But you, brothers, must live by the law of the Spirit so that you do not gratify the desires of the flesh.
Commentary on Galatians, Book Three (Galatians 5.7–6.18), 5.17 (FOTC 121)

85. What should hold first place among the fruits of the Spirit besides love? For without it the rest of the virtues are not reckoned virtues; and from love all good things are born. … No matter how hostile (by his own moral failing) someone is to a person who has love, and no matter how much he tries to dash his sense of personal peace against the waves of animosity, the one who loves remains

unshaken and never considers a creature of God worthy of hatred. For love covers a multitude of sins.
Commentary on Galatians, Book Three (Galatians 5.7–6.18), 5.22–23 (FOTC 121)

Charity—*Forgiveness*

86. Ponder well, O Christian; ponder well, O monk; if the Lord received His deadly conspirator and traitor with a kiss and prayed for those who were persecuting Him, what is our duty toward our brethren?
Homilies on the Psalms, Homily 35, Psalm 108 (109) (FOTC 48)

87. Many who measure God's commands according to their own feebleness, rather than by the strength of the saints, think that the things that have been commanded here are impossible. They say that in view of our strength, it is sufficient not to hate one's enemies; but to be commanded to love them, well, this goes beyond what is experienced by human nature. It needs to be known, therefore, that Christ does not command impossibilities, but perfection. This is what David practiced with respect to Saul and Absalom. Stephen too, the martyr, prayed for his enemies who were stoning him. Moreover, Paul desires to be accursed on behalf of his own persecutors. And Jesus both taught and practiced this when he said: "Father, forgive them; for they know not what they do" (Luke 23.34).
Commentary on Matthew, Book One (Matthew 1.1–10.42), 5.44 (FOTC 117)

Charity—*Repentance*

88. Greater by far are the wounds of the tongue than those of the sword. The sword kills the body, not the soul; the tongue kills the soul. The tongue is a bad business, a great evil … What more monstrous sin is there than blasphemy against God? Yet it is the tongue

that is sinning. Why did the devil fall? Because he committed theft? Because he committed murder? Because he committed adultery? These are certainly evils, but the devil did not fall because of any of these; he fell because of his tongue. ... Monks surely, then, have no right to think they are safe and say: We are in the monastery and so we do not commit serious offenses; I do not commit adultery; I do not steal; I am not a murderer; I am not guilty of parricide; and so of all the rest of the big vices. But the devilish sins are those of the tongue. It is outrageous to detract from my brother; I am killing my brother with my tongue ... It is no slight fault to malign a brother, to be unable to keep silence, to go from cell to cell slandering others. I am a sinner; he is a sinner; what has that to do with you? Take heed about yourself lest you fall. Why do you take pleasure in another's fall? If I fall, will you remain standing? Granted it is my downfall, but the fall of your brother ought to be your fear, not your joy. He fell. Are you glad or are you sorry? Answer me. A brother has fallen into sin; either you rejoice or you are sorry. If you are glad, does one rejoice in the misfortune of another? If you are sorry, why do you go about gossiping? Why do you tell others? Let God see your sorrow, and let the brother himself perceive it; do not let other brethren hear about it.

Homilies on the Psalms, Homily 41, Psalm 119 (120) (FOTC 48)

89. If an enemy slanders you, he does you no harm; you slay yourself if you slander others. By way of example, if a brother blackens me, what harm does he do me? If he should call me a murderer, and adulterer, a scoundrel, a liar, what wrong does he do me? He is doing one of two things certainly: either he is telling the truth or he is telling a lie. If he is telling the truth, what he has said does not hurt me; but the fact that I have really committed the act, that does. If, however, he is lying, his lie does not injure me, but it kills the soul of the one uttering it. Unhappy men that we are, what miserable creatures! When we have an enemy and think that we are doing something against him, all the while we are doing it against ourselves. We disparage him; we go hither and thither talking about

him to everybody. Do we think that we are hurting him? We are doing nothing to him, but we are killing our own souls because we are lying.
Homilies on the Psalms, Homily 41, Psalm 119 (120) (FOTC 48)

CHARITY—*The Virtue of Love*

90. All men are our neighbor, and we should not harm anyone. If, on the contrary, we understand our fellow man to be only our brother and relatives, is it then permitted us to do evil to strangers? God forbid such belief! We are neighbors, all men to all men, for we have one father.
Homilies on the Psalms, Homily 5, Psalm 14 (15) (FOTC 48)

91. Fear is the mark of beginners; love, the sign of the perfect.
Homilies on the Psalms, Homily 6, Psalm 66 (67) (FOTC 48)

92. See how much love, how much yearning pierces the soul of the saint in the courts of the Lord!
Homilies on the Psalms: Second Series, Homily 63, Psalm 83 (84) (FOTC 57)

CHARITY—*Works*

93. The Word of the Lord does not come by the hand but by the mouth, but grasp the mysticism of Scripture. God does not come because of words, but because of good works. ... {God} heeds works, that words may be translated into works.
Homilies on the Psalms, Homily 46, Psalm 133 (134) (FOTC 48)

94. You will find some Christians giving alms in order to be honored by men. When a poor beggar comes up to them, such Christians first

look all around and, unless they catch sight of a witness, they do not give their money. If that kind of person is alone, his hand is cramped even more than ever; he does not give willingly. O you Christian, a pauper begs you for money, why do you refuse him in secret but give to him in public? If you seek God as your witness, why do you look around for human eyes? Your almsgiving in the presence of the unsophisticated looks like real almsgiving, but in the presence of God it is a wrong; you are doing an injury to your brother, for you wish to show him up as a beggar in the presence of others. When we have the opportunity of giving, therefore, let us give not as from our own substance, but as from Christ's; we ought not give as to a beggar, but as to a brother. We give him material things; he gives us spiritual; the pauper gives more than he receives. We give him bread that will be consumed that same day; in return for the bread, he gives us the kingdom of heaven.

Homilies on the Psalms, Homily 46, Psalm 133 (134) (FOTC 48)

95. If we can please both God and others at the same time, let us also please others. If we can please others only by displeasing God, then our priority must be to please God.

Commentary on Galatians, Book One (Galatians 1.1–3.9), 1.10 (FOTC 121)

96. This does not mean that the works of the Law ought to be discarded and that a one-dimensional faith devoid of works is the goal. It means rather that faith in Christ enriches these works. Indeed, that saying of the wise man is well known, "The faithful man does not live by righteousness, but the righteousman lives by faith" (Hab 2:4).

Commentary on Galatians, Book One (Galatians 1.1–3.9), 3.5 (FOTC 121)

97. It is evident that the expression of faith through love embodies the completeness of all of the commandments. Just as faith without works is dead, as the Apostle James says (cf. James 2.26), so works, even though they be good, are counted as dead without faith. What do unbelievers with good morals have besides the [empty] works of virtue? *Commentary on Galatians*, Book Two (Galatians 3.10–5.6), 5.6 (FOTC 121)

Chastity

CHASTITY—*The Eucharist*

98. If we intend, therefore, to eat the flesh of the lamb, we must mortify our loins, the works of the flesh … We must not permit the flesh to lust against the spirit, but, with the spirit, mortify the deeds of the flesh and, thus purified, enjoy the flesh of the lamb.
Various Homilies: Second Series, Homily 91—On the Exodus (*The Vigil of Easter*) (FOTC 57)

CHASTITY—*Fallenness*

99. The only difference between a fornicator and detractor is, moreover, that the fornicator slays only himself, but the slanderer ruins both himself and the one who listens to him.
Homilies on the Psalms, Homily 27, Psalm 100 (101) (FOTC 48)

CHASTITY—*Freedom*

100. The Gospel commands things that we are able to do, for example, that we should not lust. This lies within our choice.
Commentary on Matthew, Book Two (Matthew 11.2–16.12), 11.30 (FOTC 117)

101. We may add something to Origen's exposition. Those to whom it was said above, "Stand firm and do not let yourselves be burdened again by a yoke of slavery" (cf. Galatians 5.1)—are being warned now not to think by any means that they can use this freedom as a license to indulge in the flesh... as they pursue the light yoke of Christ and the Gospel's delectable commandments (cf. 1 John 5.3). ... Someone may say: So, Paul, if I am no longer under the Law and have been called from slavery to freedom, then I must live in a way that does justice to this freedom and not be bound by any commandments. Whatever tickles my fancy and whatever desire suggests to me, that I must do, that I must fulfill, that I must chase after. The Apostle's response is that we are indeed called to freedom of the Spirit, provided that it does not entail slavery to the flesh. We should not think that everything is expedient just because everything is permissible (cf. 1 Corinthians 6.13, 10.23).
Commentary on Galatians, Book Three (Galatians 5.7–6.18), 5.13a (FOTC 121)

102. The flesh delights in what is present and fleeting, the Spirit in the eternal and in future things. ... It takes enormous effort and discrimination to scrutinize the deeds of the flesh and the deeds of the Spirit and to pinpoint specific ones that seem to be neither fleshly nor spiritual but somewhere in between. We are said to be carnal when we surrender ourselves to pleasures, and spiritual when we follow the Holy Spirit's lead, that is, when we gain wisdom from his guidance and take him as our teacher. ... But I beg you not to use your freedom as an excuse to do whatever you please, not to think that everything which is permissible will be of benefit to you, and not to indulge in debauchery.
Commentary on Galatians, Book Three (Galatians 5.7–6.18), 5.17 (FOTC 121)

CHASTITY—*Grace*

103. What nature failed to subjugate in us, grace subdues.
Homilies on the Psalms: Second Series, Homily 71, Psalm 93 (94) (FOTC 57)

CHASTITY—*The Priesthood*

104. The true priest, therefore, must have… the power of communication, that he may bring forth and impart to others, what he conceives in his mind and heart. Yet all these powers are vain if chastity has not been a precaution and an adornment.
Homilies on the Psalms, Homily 45, Psalm 132 (133) (FOTC 48)

CHASTITY—*Sacrifice*

105. All chastity, whether in virginity, widowhood, or continence, is a sacrificial offering to Christ. I am going to mention a new thought here: chastity is the sacrificial gift that brings and gives itself.
Homilies on the Psalms, Homily 23, Psalm 95 (96) (FOTC 48)

CHASTITY—*Salvation*

106. When the adulterer is saved, he is saved not as adulterer, but as the just and chaste.
Homilies on the Psalms: Second Series, Homily 62, Psalm 82 (83) (FOTC 57)

107. The one who puts no confidence in the flesh looks to Christ for all benefit and does not sow [to please] his sinful nature, only to reap destruction from that nature. He instead sows [to please] the Spirit, from whom eternal life comes.
Commentary on Galatians, Book Two (Galatians 3.10–5.6), 5.2 (FOTC 121)

CHASTITY—*Temptation*

108. If the spirit slips, how much more the body, which is more prone toward sins.
Commentary on Matthew, Book One (Matthew 1.1–10.42), 5.29 (FOTC 117)

Conversion

CONVERSION—*Conscience*

109. It is a good thing to sing a sacred song. To sing, not with the voice, mind you, but with the heart. How many there are who have good voices but because they are sinners, their singing is bad. He sings well who sings in his heart, who sings to Christ in his conscience. ... It is fitting to praise Him with joyful song, not with the voice, but with a good conscience.
Homilies on the Psalms, Homily 56, Psalm 146 (147A) (FOTC 48)

CONVERSION—*Faith*

110. Christ, the victor over demons and vices, enters more directly and securely into the hearts of believers.
Commentary on Matthew, Book Three (Matthew 16.13–22.40), 21.8 (FOTC 117)

CONVERSION—*Forgiveness*

111. Let this be the prayer of the sinner, in view of the fact that he has obtained pardon: Lord, you have blessed this clay of Yours. Even though it has brought forth thistles and thorns, it is, nevertheless, Your creature and for that reason has been restored.
Homilies on the Psalms, Homily 17, Psalm 84 (85) (FOTC 48)

CONVERSION—*Healing*

112. Just as the good and kind doctor rejoices with his patient when he has cured him, so also does our Lord.
Homilies on the Psalms, Homily 34, Psalm 107 (108) (FOTC 48)

113. If a physician should notice infected and decayed tissue in a body and say, "What concern is that of mine?" you would conclude rightly that he is cruel; but if he should excise the infected tissues and cauterize the wound, he is compassionate, for he is saving the life of a man. Likewise, a teacher, if he dismisses a lad and does not exact obedience from him, hates him; if, on the other hand, he disciplines him and the remedy cures him, his apparent severity turns out to be clemency.
Homilies on the Psalms, Homily 51, Psalm 140 (141) (FOTC 48)

CONVERSION—*The Holy Spirit*

114. Let us pray to the Lord that any hardness in us may soften, that our sins be purged, that we may become as fire, so the chill of the devil—whatever there is of it in our hearts—may be expelled, so that we may grow warm with the Holy Spirit.
Homilies on the Psalms, Homily 57, Psalm 147 (147B) (FOTC 48)

CONVERSION—*Hope*

115. If you are a sinner, do not despair; if you are just, do not yield to complacency.
Homilies on the Psalms, Homily 17, Psalm 84 (85) (FOTC 48)

116. As long as we continue in a life of sin, we certainly are not trusting; if we put an end to sin, then our hope is confident.
Homilies on the Psalms, Homily 20, Psalm 90 (91) (FOTC 48)

117. May the sun of Christ rise in your soul always that always a new light may shine in you.
Homilies on the Psalms, Homily 23, Psalm 95 (96) (FOTC 48)

CONVERSION—*Mercy*

118. There is no time when mercy shall not be built up in each and every one of the saints, and in those who make the change from sin to virtues.
The Dialogue Against the Pelagians, Book Two, paragraph 20 (FOTC 53)

CONVERSION—*Patience*

119. If you aim an arrow at a stone, and the stone is hard, not only will the arrow fail to penetrate, but it will even rebound. It is the same with your enemy; if he should strike you and you do not retaliate, he will be conquered by your patience and you will convert him.
Homilies on the Psalms, Homily 22, Psalm 93 (94) (FOTC 48)

CONVERSION—*Peace*

120. When they will have ceased to be enemies, then You, O Lord, will be exalted among them.
Homilies on the Psalms, Homily 3, Psalm 7 (FOTC 48)

CONVERSION—*Purity*

121. Take away, O Lord, my uncleanness; take away whatever there is of baseness. Grant Your snow, Your purity, to the minds and hearts of Christians. Unless You cleanse us with the snow of Your purity, we cannot wear Your garment. Christ is our garment. If we want to possess Christ as our garment, let us be pure as snow.
Homilies on the Psalms, Homily 57, Psalm 147 (147B) (FOTC 48)

CONVERSION—*Repentance*

122. We cry to God with our hands as many times as we cry to him with our tears.
Homilies on the Psalms, Homily 10, Psalm 76 (77) (FOTC 48)

123. Yesterday a thief, today a Christian; yesterday a fornicator, today continent; yesterday you were plundering the goods of others; today you are offering your own.
Homilies on the Psalms, Homily 10, Psalm 76 (77) (FOTC 48)

124. We are at the beginning, not at the end of perfection.
Homilies on the Psalms, Homily 21, Psalm 91 (92) (FOTC 48)

125. O, you, who before had been subject to the dominion of the lord devil, are now subject to the rule of the Lord Creator.
Homilies on the Psalms, Homily 24, Psalm 96 (97) (FOTC 48)

126. Without any doubt, it is the Lord who contrives snares for sinners themselves, in order to entrap those who abuse their freedom and to compel them to tread the right path under his bridle, thereby making it possible for them to advance through him who says: "I am the way" (John 14:6a).
Homilies on the Psalms: Second Series, Homily 60, Psalm 10 (11) (FOTC 57)

127. The Lord went to the banquets of sinners, in order to have an opportunity to teach and in order to offer spiritual food to those who had invited him. After all, when he is described as going frequently to the banquets, nothing else is related except what he did and taught there. Thus both the humility of the Lord in going to sinners and the power of his teaching in the conversion of the repentant are demonstrated.
Commentary on Matthew, Book One (Matthew 1.1–10.42), 9.13 (FOTC 117)

CONVERSION—*The Resurrection*

128. Until the Lord restores us to life, we are dead.
Homilies on the Psalms, Homily 17, Psalm 84 (85) (FOTC 48)

CONVERSION—*Salvation*

129. May the enemies of God not perish, but lay aside their hardness and be converted unto repentance and be saved.
Homilies on the Psalms, Homily 7, Psalm 67 (68) (FOTC 48)

130. He is pleading, not against them, but for their salvation.
Homilies on the Psalms, Homily 15, Psalm 82 (83) (FOTC 48)

131. No one should despair of salvation if he is converted to better things.
Commentary on Matthew, Book One (Matthew 1.1–10.42), 9.9 (FOTC 117)

CONVERSION—*Wisdom*

132. Because I have begun to exhort you to leave behind childish elements, syllables, and reading habits and to aspire to more advanced things, so that you may hold books in your hands and learn words full of wisdom and meaningfulness, you rebel, you become angry, and the idea of doctrinal enlightenment seems burdensome to you. ... That proverb of the poet who is considered noble among the Romans is apt here, "Flattery attracts friends, and truth, hatred" (cf. Terence, *Andria* 68).
Commentary on Galatians, Book Two (Galatians 3.10–5.6), 4.15–16 (FOTC 121)

Divine Revelation

DIVINE REVELATION—*Creation*

133. When the people crossed the Red Sea and the River Jordan, the waters recognized their creator, but the people did not.
Homilies on the Psalms, Homily 10, Psalm 76 (77) (FOTC 48)

134. Because there is no one like You, we look for no other Creator except You.
Homilies on the Psalms, Homily 15, Psalm 82 (83) (FOTC 48)

135. That is the very distinction that separates us from brutes and beasts—that we recognize our Creator.
Homilies on the Psalms, Homily 54, Psalm 143 (144) (FOTC 48)

DIVINE REVELATION—*Evangelization*

136. The sign of the Lord's coming is the proclamation of the Gospel in the whole world. Thus no one will have an excuse.
Commentary on Matthew, Book Four (Matthew 22.41–28.20), 24.14 (FOTC 117)

137. Before the Gospel of Christ had shone throughout the entire world, the commandments of the Law had their own luster. But after the greater light from evangelical grace shone and the sun of righteousness revealed itself to the whole world, the light from the stars was concealed and their rays grew dark.
Commentary on Galatians, Book Two (Galatians 3.10–5.6), 4.8–9 (FOTC 121)

DIVINE REVELATION—*Faith*

138. To have perceived there is a God is to have believed; to acknowledge God is to honor Him.
Homilies on the Psalms, Homily 26, Psalm 98 (99) (FOTC 48)

139. Panic persists in those in whom abides unbelief.
Commentary on Matthew, Book Four (Matthew 22.41–28.20), 28.4–5 (FOTC 117)

DIVINE REVELATION—*Grace*

140. After Peter's denial and the crowing of the cock, the Savior looked at Peter, and by his gaze he provoked him to bitter tears. For it was impossible for one on whom the Light of the world had looked to remain in the darkness of denial.
Commentary on Matthew, Book Four (Matthew 22.41–28.20), 26.74 (FOTC 117)

DIVINE REVELATION—*History*

141. Josephus in the eighteenth book of his *Antiquities* most clearly states that Christ was put to death by the Pharisees because of the greatness of his miracles, and that John the Baptist was a true prophet, and that Jerusalem was subjected to destruction because James the apostle had been put to death.
On Illustrious Men, XIII. Josephus, Son of Matthew, 4 (FOTC 100)

DIVINE REVELATION—*The Incarnation*

142. Before the Lord came in the flesh, there was inequality, for God was known only in Judea. He came, and all the earth recognized the

one and same Creator that Judea had known, and the correction of His throne was accomplished.
Homilies on the Psalms: Second Series, Homily 73, Psalm 96 (97) (FOTC 57)

143. Christ is not found except by the vigilant.
Various Homilies, Homily 88—On the Nativity of the Lord (FOTC 57)

144. It is one thing not to believe in one who is coming, but it is something else not to receive him who has come.
Commentary on Matthew, Book Two (Matthew 11.2–16.12), 12.44 (FOTC 117)

DIVINE REVELATION—*Joy*

145. If the hearts of those who seek the Lord are full of joy, how much more the hearts of those who find Him?
Homilies on the Psalms, Homily 31, Psalm 104 (105) (FOTC 48)

DIVINE REVELATION—*Judaism and the Holy Land*

146. The Jews are the first son; we are the last ones.
Homilies on the Psalms, Homily 4, Psalm 9 (9a-9b) (FOTC 48)

147. God was renowned in Juda, in Israel great was His name. Knowledge of God's name was heralded to a moderate part of the earth.
Homilies on the Psalms, Homily 14, Psalm 81 (82) (FOTC 48)

148. Happy the man who bears in his heart the cross and the Resurrection, the place of Christ's Nativity, and the place of is Ascension! Happy the man who has Bethlehem in his heart, in whose heart Christ is born every day!
Homilies on the Psalms, Homily 23, Psalm 95 (96) (FOTC 48)

149. We have been grafted upon [the root of the Jews]; we are the branches, they the root. We must not curse our roots.
Homilies on the Psalms, Homily 35, Psalm 108 (109) (FOTC 48)

150. Wonderful things are said to have been accomplished only in the land of God.
Homilies on the Psalms: Second Series, Homily 61, Psalm 15 (16) (FOTC 57)

151. There was nothing sublime nor lofty there [in Galilee] before the coming of the Savior; everything base was tolerated: luxury, filth, impurities, the wallowing place for the muck of swine.
Homilies on the Gospel of Saint Mark on Various Topics, Homily 76 (II)—On Mark 1.13–31 (FOTC 57)

DIVINE REVELATION—*Miracles*

152. God is awesome because he so loves the human race that he performs miracles through his saints. He is more awesome in his saints than in the rest of his creatures.
Homilies on the Psalms, Homily 7, Psalm 67 (68) (FOTC 48)

153. O wondrous deed communicating sublime secrets!
Homilies on the Psalms, Homily 13, Psalm 80 (81) (FOTC 48)

154. They demand a sign, as if the signs that they had seen did not exist.
Commentary on Matthew, Book Two (Matthew 11.2–16.12), 12.38 (FOTC 117)

DIVINE REVELATION—*The Natural World*

155. The God of all through nature has become our God personally.
Homilies on the Psalms, Homily 6, Psalm 66 (67) (FOTC 48)

156. There is no nation that does not naturally know there is a God.
Homilies on the Psalms, Homily 23, Psalm 95 (96) (FOTC 48)

157. Is it not cause for wonderment when, moreover, we behold the elephant and the camels on the one hand, and the fly and the mosquito on the other, all with the same mobility, breath of life, and members?
Homilies on the Psalms, Homily 37, Psalm 110 (111) (FOTC 48)

DIVINE REVELATION—*The Parousia*

158. No small amount of time passes between the first and the second coming of the Lord.
Commentary on Matthew, Book Four (Matthew 22.41–28.20), 25.5 (FOTC 117)

DIVINE REVELATION—*Praise*

159. To praise God, human nature alone does not suffice; the heavens, too, join in his praise.
Homilies on the Psalms, Homily 58, Psalm 148 (FOTC 48)

160. Take note, heathens; note well, Manichaeans. The sun gives praise, it does not receive it.
Homilies on the Psalms, Homily 58, Psalm 148 (FOTC 48)

DIVINE REVELATION—*Redemption*

161. The Lord who always was, has become my stronghold; therefore, the Savior who always was, has become my Redeemer.
Homilies on the Psalms, Homily 22, Psalm 93 (94) (FOTC 48)

162. The prophecy of our Lord Savior {is} evident, not only in word, but also in deed.
Homilies on the Psalms: Second Series, Homily 61, Psalm 15 (16) (FOTC 57)

163. {Jesus} bathed in brilliant light all those blinded by the darkness of sin.
Homilies on the Psalms: Second Series, Fragment of Homily 74, Psalm 93 (94)—Easter Homily (FOTC 57)

DIVINE REVELATION—*Sovereignty*

164. If, moreover, he is said to be the Most High Lord, how much the more is he the Word of God?
Homilies on the Psalms, Homily 18, Psalm 86 (87) (FOTC 48)

165. As with these eyes of ours we cannot look into an unfathomable depth, neither are we able to contemplate the majesty nor the wisdom of God.
Homilies on the Psalms, Homily 30, Psalm 103 (104) (FOTC 48)

166. "O God, who is like You?" No one is like You.
Homilies on the Psalms: Second Series, Homily 62, Psalm 82 (83) (FOTC 57)

167. Not the numberless multitude of false gods, but you alone are the Most High over all the earth.
Homilies on the Psalms: Second Series, Homily 62, Psalm 82 (83) (FOTC 57)

168. After preaching and teaching {Jesus} would cure every kind of disease and infirmity, so that his works might persuade those whom his words had not persuaded.
Commentary on Matthew, Book One (Matthew 1.1–10.42), 9.35 (FOTC 117)

169. Thus the greatness of the signs will prove the greatness of the promises.
Commentary on Matthew, Book One (Matthew 1.1–10.42), 10.7–8 (FOTC 117)

170. In comparison with the true light, all things will seem dark.
Commentary on Matthew, Book Four (Matthew 22.41–28.20), 24.29 (FOTC 117)

Doctrine

DOCTRINE—*Conscience*

171. When our lamentation and our conscience entreat the Lord, this is the cry that God heeds.
Homilies on the Psalms, Homily 2, Psalm 5 (FOTC 48)

172. He who says: "Be not silent, O God," is at peace with his conscience.
Homilies on the Psalms, Homily 15, Psalm 82 (83) (FOTC 48)

173. Wherever there is a damaged conscience, sins of the tongue abound.
Homilies on the Psalms, Homily 22, Psalm 93 (94) (FOTC 48)

174. Who of us is the strong ship that can escape shipwreck in this world and not be sunk or dashed against a rock, but has a conscience to steer him so that he may be safe?
Homilies on the Psalms, Homily 30, Psalm 103 (104) (FOTC 48)

DOCTRINE—*Contemplation*

175. It is not enough to want the law of God, but one must meditate on his law day and night (cf. Psalm 1.2).
Homilies on the Psalms, Homily 1, Psalm 1 (FOTC 48)

DOCTRINE—*Courage*

176. First, fear is expelled so that afterward, doctrine may be imparted.
Commentary on Matthew, Book Three (Matthew 16.13–22.40), 17.7 (FOTC 117)

DOCTRINE—*Discipleship*

177. Under your spiritual law, and under your spiritual priesthood, you have guided us, your people.
Homilies on the Psalms, Homily 10, Psalm 76 (77) (FOTC 48)

178. Cause for wonder it is, indeed, to hear the roar of the sea and its raging fury and the howl of the waves lashed as high as the sky, and see them rush in as if to submerge the entire world, hurl their full force as far as the shore, and then recede and not transgress the frontiers appointed by God—yet men do not keep the commandments of God.
Homilies on the Psalms, Homily 30, Psalm 103 (104) (FOTC 48)

DOCTRINE—*Evangelization*

179. Even the things that are thought to be least in the law are full of spiritual mysteries, and … all things are recapitulated in the gospel.
Commentary on Matthew, Book One (Matthew 1.1–10.42), 5.18 (FOTC 117)

180. {Christ} died to the original Law through the Law of the Gospel. And the soul, which according to the epistle to the Romans would be called an adulteress if she remarried while her first husband was still alive, wed the spiritual Law so that she might bear fruit for God, when her husband, the old Law, died (cf. Rom 7.2–4).
Commentary on Galatians, Book One (Galatians 1.1–3.9), 2.19a (FOTC 121)

181. Since the world did not have the wisdom to recognize God from the orderliness, diversity, and constancy of his creatures, God saw fit to save those who believed through the foolishness of the Gospel message. He accomplished this neither through the persuasive words of worldly wisdom nor through clever eloquence, lest the cross of Christ be emptied of its potency (cf. 1 Corinthians 1.17); where is the wise man, where is the grammarian, where are the natural scientists? [God] accomplished this rather through the display of power and the Spirit, so that the faith of believers might rest in the power of God, and not in the wisdom of men.
Commentary on Galatians, Book Three (Galatians 5.7–6.18), Preface (FOTC 121)

DOCTRINE—*God's Will*

182. In the same way that one thirsts in the midday heat, this loyal servant thirsts and longs to obey the commands of the Lord. He bears great love always in fulfilling the Lord's will. He does not merely do his bidding, he wills it, not just in passing, but with all the ardor of his heart.
Homilies on the Psalms, Homily 38, Psalm 111 (112) (FOTC 48)

DOCTRINE—*Growth*

183. In the realm of doctrine, there are individual steps that lead to the attainment of happiness.
Commentary on Galatians, Book Two (Galatians 3.10–5.6), 4.15–16 (FOTC 121)

DOCTRINE—*Love*

184. The man who fears the Lord, the happy man, cheerfully obeys the commands of the Lord; He loves His commands with a deep and strong love. Grasp what that means.
Homilies on the Psalms, Homily 38, Psalm 111 (112) (FOTC 48)

DOCTRINE—*Righteousness*

185. This natural law can then be augmented by observance of the Law and the righteousness that comes from the Law—not the fleshly law, which has passed away, but the spiritual Law, for the Law is spiritual.
Commentary on Galatians, Book One (Galatians 1.1–3.9), 3.2 (FOTC 121)

DOCTRINE—*Scandal*

186. Every teacher who scandalizes his disciples by his evil works shuts the kingdom of heaven before them.
Commentary on Matthew, Book Four (Matthew 22.41–28.20), 23.13 (FOTC 117)

DOCTRINE—*Understanding*

187. Anyone who is unworthy is unable to comprehend divine doctrine; for him it is covered over with clouds.
Homilies on the Psalms, Homily 56, Psalm 146 (147A) (FOTC 48)

188. The law must be taught in order that its obscurities may be carefully cleared away.
Homilies on the Psalms: Second Series, Homily 71, Psalm 93 (94) (FOTC 57)

189. If there are strong things in [Sacred Scripture], such as the Church's dogma on the Trinity, the Resurrection, the soul, the angels, and other matters of this kind, we should not argue about them and cling to opinions based on distorted interpretations and pound them to pieces; but state them exactly as the strong doctrine that they are.
Various Homilies, Homily 91—On the Exodus (*The Vigil of Easter*) (FOTC 57)

190. The laws of God are never contrary to one another.
Commentary on Matthew, Book Two (Matthew 11.2–16.12), 12.5 (FOTC 117)

DOCTRINE—*Virtue*

191. There are many who observe the law through fear, but fear as a motive for action is far from meritorious.
Homilies on the Psalms, Homily 1, Psalm 1 (FOTC 48)

192. Meditation on the law does not consist in reading, but in doing, just as the Apostle says in another place: "Whether you eat or drink, or do anything else, do all for the glory of God" (1 Corinthians 10.31). Even if I merely stretch forth my hand in almsgiving, I am meditating on the law of God; if I visit the sick, my feet are meditating on the law of God; if I do what is prescribed, I am praying with my whole body what others are praying with their lips.
Homilies on the Psalms, Homily 1, Psalm 1 (FOTC 48)

Eternity

ETERNITY—*Earthly Life*

193. Compared to the eternity of God, man's whole lifespan is brief; however long it may seem to us, in comparison to eternity, it is reckoned as nothing, for it comes to an end.

Homilies on the Psalms: Second Series, Homily 67, Psalm 89 (90) (FOTC 57)

194. Just as quickly as the morning dew disappears, so passes the life of man.
Homilies on the Psalms: Second Series, Homily 67, Psalm 89 (90) (FOTC 57)

ETERNITY—*Eschatology*

195. Our inheritance is not promised at the beginning, but at the end of the world.
Homilies on the Psalms, Homily 2, Psalm 5 (FOTC 48)

ETERNITY—*Eternal Life*

196. The Lord does not have the weapons of death, but the instruments of life.
Homilies on the Psalms, Homily 3, Psalm 7 (FOTC 48)

197. Now the churches that you see are tabernacles, for we are not here as permanent dwellers, but rather as those about to migrate to another place.
Homilies on the Psalms, Homily 5, Psalm 14 (15) (FOTC 48)

198. We do not remain as dwellers, but as pilgrims.
Homilies on the Psalms, Homily 16, Psalm 83 (84) (FOTC 48)

199. In one place we are planted; in another place we flourish; here we are planted; in the kingdom of God we shall flourish.
Homilies on the Psalms, Homily 21, Psalm 91 (92) (FOTC 48)

200. As long as we tarry in this bodily tent of ours, we are wanderers away from the Lord. … In the present world we have no lasting dwelling place; we are pilgrims.
Homilies on the Psalms, Homily 41, Psalm 119 (120) (FOTC 48)

201. The soul and the body both share in longing for the kingdom of heaven.
Homilies on the Psalms: Second Series, Homily 63, Psalm 83 (84) (FOTC 57)

202. We are hastening on our way to heaven, for here we do not have a lasting place, but we are wayfarers and pilgrims, like all our fathers.
Homilies on the Psalms: Second Series, Homily 63, Psalm 83 (84) (FOTC 57)

203. If, therefore, sparrows seek their nests, why should not the human soul seek the dwelling place prepared for it by the Lord?
Homilies on the Psalms: Second Series, Homily 63, Psalm 83 (84) (FOTC 57)

ETERNITY—*Free Will*

204. How much more should men be directed by the choice of God, men to whom eternity is promised.
Commentary on Matthew, Book One (Matthew 1.1–10.42), 6.26 (FOTC 117)

ETERNITY—*Glory*

205. If the glory of the Lord endures forever, we, too, who glorify him will be everlasting.
Homilies on the Psalms, Homily 30, Psalm 103 (104) (FOTC 48)

ETERNITY—*Goodness*

206. Nothing is good save the eternal; nothing is good except the everlasting. Anything that is finite is not to be counted among the good. What good does it do me if yesterday I feasted and today I am dying of

hunger? What good to me if in the days gone by I was a king and today I am dying in prison? Whatever is passing and has an end is nothing.
Homilies on the Psalms, Homily 21, Psalm 91 (92) (FOTC 48)

207. Reminiscence brings more pain than pleasure. Nothing is good except that which lasts forever.
Homilies on the Psalms, Homily 21, Psalm 91 (92) (FOTC 48)

208. Let us beg the Lord that everything that we have said—both that which we have said and that which you have heard—we may fulfill in good works; that we may translate words into works; that we, who have been planted here in the house of the Lord, may flourish there in the court of Christ.
Homilies on the Psalms, Homily 21, Psalm 91 (92) (FOTC 48)

ETERNITY—*Happiness*

209. Fruitful and happy the mind and heart that day and night are filled with longing for the dwelling place of the Lord!
Homilies on the Psalms: Second Series, Homily 63, Psalm 83 (84) (FOTC 57)

ETERNITY—*Joy*

210. For the reason that in the present world no matter how faithful one may be, no matter to what degree one renounces the world, his is not a perfect victory. ... It is evident that in the present world there is no lasting joy; our joy is only ephemeral.
Homilies on the Psalms, Homily 18, Psalm 86 (87) (FOTC 48)

ETERNITY—*Judgment*

211. Consider the bee or the ant; see its body and search into its wisdom—a wisdom far greater than the magnitude of its body! Bees

and ants plan ahead for the winter that is to come, but the monk and the Christian give no thought to the judgment that is on its way. The bee and the ant know that they can be imperiled by hunger if they do not labor in the summertime for the winter supply of food; we do not reflect that without good works we shall be tormented in hell.
Homilies on the Psalms, Homily 21, Psalm 91 (92) (FOTC 48)

Evangelization

EVANGELIZATION—*The Apostle Paul*

212. Although the cults of idolatry had multiplied, at the first sound of {Paul} the Apostle's voice, the Gentiles believed and turned to the Lord.
Homilies on the Psalms: Second Series, Homily 61, Psalm 15 (16) (FOTC 57)

213. Nowadays in churches, the purity and simplicity of {Paul} the Apostle's words are done away with, and other qualities are in demand. We congregate as if we were in the Athenaeum or in lecture halls and we long for the thundering applause of bystanders and a speech that, like a dolled-up harlot strolling in the streets, is decorated in the deceit of rhetorical artifice, and aims to win the favor of the masses rather than to instruct them, soothing the ears of the listeners like a sweet-sounding psaltery and flute.
Commentary on Galatians, Book Three (Galatians 5.7–6.18), Preface (FOTC 121)

EVANGELIZATION—*Apostolic Succession*

214. The apostles led the way followed by those who have believed through them—or, undoubtedly, by the churches.
Homilies on the Psalms, Homily 7, Psalm 67 (68) (FOTC 48)

215. The Lord is either in light or he is in darkness. He is in light for beginners, for he speaks more plainly to them; but to the proficient, he speaks mystically. He did not speak to the apostles in the same way that he spoke to the multitudes; he spoke to the apostles esoterically. *Homilies on the Psalms*, Homily 24, Psalm 96 (97) (FOTC 48)

216. These were the first ones to be called to follow the Lord. They are illiterate fishermen and are sent to preach, lest it be thought that the faith of believers comes from eloquence and learning rather than from the power of God.
Commentary on Matthew, Book One (Matthew 1.1–10.42), 4.19 (FOTC 117)

EVANGELIZATION—*Baptism*

217. If we are Christians (we, who have received the baptism of Christ are, indeed, Christians and not only confess but profess that we are), because we are Christians, we must believe the evangelists. *Homilies on the Psalms*, Homily 11, Psalm 77 (78) (FOTC 48)

EVANGELIZATION—*Discipleship*

218. The way, the life, and the truth is Christ (cf. John 14.6); let us walk, therefore, in Christ and then God the Father will know our way. *Homilies on the Psalms*, Homily 1, Psalm 1 (FOTC 48)

219. When a teacher instructs a student, unless he himself believes what he is teaching, he cannot teach the other. *Homilies on the Psalms*, Homily 40, Psalm 115 (116B) (FOTC 48)

220. Saints receive from the mouth of God the two-edged swords that they hold in their hands. The Lord... gives the sword from his mouth to his disciples; a two-edged sword, namely, the word of his teachings; a two-edged sword, historically and allegorically, the letter

and the spirit; a two-edged sword that slays adversaries and at the same time defends his faithful. ... This two-edged sword has two heads: it speaks of the present and of the future world; here, it strikes down adversaries; above, it opens up the kingdom of heaven.
Homilies on the Psalms, Homily 59, Psalm 149 (FOTC 48)

221. Unless there was something divinely compelling in the face of the Savior, they acted irrationally in following a man whom they had never seen before. Does one leave a father to follow a man in whom he sees nothing more than in his father? They leave their father of the flesh to follow the Father of the spirit; they do not leave a father, they find a Father. What is the point of this digression? To show that there was something divine in the Savior's countenance that men, seeing, could not resist. ... [The disciple] Matthew sees no miracle; the authority in the One calling him was the miracle.
Homilies on the Gospel of Saint Mark on Various Topics, Homily 83 (IX)—On Mark 11.15–17 (FOTC 57)

222. Authority has been given "in heaven and on earth." Thus he who was previously reigning in heaven reigns on earth through the faith of believers.
Commentary on Matthew, Book Four (Matthew 22.41–28.20), 28.18 (FOTC 117)

223. The work of God is, of course, one thing, the work of men another. God's work is to call, and men's work is either to believe or not to believe.
Commentary on Galatians, Book Three (Galatians 5.7–6.18), 5.8 (FOTC 121)

EVANGELIZATION—*Faith*

224. True faith does not hesitate; it responds at once, believes at once, it follows at once, becomes a fisherman at once.
Homilies on the Gospel of Saint Mark on Various Topics, Homily 76 (II)—On Mark 1.13–31 (FOTC 57)

EVANGELIZATION—*Sacred Scripture*

225. We cannot keep secret the words of our Lord.
Homilies on the Psalms, Homily 19, Psalm 89 (90) (FOTC 48)

EVANGELIZATION—*Salvation*

226. His salvation is known among all nations. Wherever human speech is able to penetrate, there resounds the name of Jesus.
Homilies on the Psalms, Homily 6, Psalm 66 (67) (FOTC 48)

227. You see that {Jesus} preached the Gospel equally in the country and in cities and villages, that is, to both the great and the small. Thus, he did not consider the power of the noble, but the salvation of believers.
Commentary on Matthew, Book One (Matthew 1.1–10.42), 9.35 (FOTC 117)

EVANGELIZATION—*Sovereignty*

228. Never is Your concern reserved only for the people of one nation; You are the God of all.
Homilies on the Psalms, Homily 6, Psalm 66 (67) (FOTC 48)

229. Mark well the swiftness of the Word; it is not satisfied with the East; it desires to speed to the West.
Homilies on the Psalms, Homily 57, Psalm 147 (147B) (FOTC 48)

EVANGELIZATION—*Truth*

230. There is to be no distinction between the noble and the ignoble, between the rich and the needy, in the proclamation of the Gospel. These things prove the rigor of the teacher and they prove the truth

of the preacher, since with him everyone is equal who can be saved.
Commentary on Matthew, Book Two (Matthew 11.2–16.12), 11.4–5
(FOTC 117)

EVANGELIZATION—*Vineyard Imagery*

231. There are no wine presses except where there is a vineyard and
a plentiful harvest of grapes.
Homilies on the Psalms, Homily 13, Psalm 80 (81) (FOTC 48)

EVANGELIZATION—*Vocations*

232. Our Lord Jesus Christ has a great household. He has those who
minister to him in his presence, and he has others who serve him
in the fields. Monks and virgins, I think, are they who attend their
Lord personally; laymen are the members of the household who are
at work in the fields.
Homilies on the Psalms, Homily 46, Psalm 133 (134) (FOTC 48)

233. Our very purpose in coming to the monastery, in giving up the
freedom of the world, is to accept the servitude of Christ.
Various Homilies, Homily 95—On Obedience (FOTC 57)

Grace and Providence

GRACE AND PROVIDENCE—*Cooperation*

234. God will bear our burdens for us. God helps us and works
with us.
Homilies on the Psalms, Homily 7, Psalm 67 (68) (FOTC 48)

235. All that is necessary is to be God's people.
Homilies on the Psalms, Homily 15, Psalm 82 (83) (FOTC 48)

236. God is our helper. While we labor with determination, he delivers us and works together with us; when we are slothful, supine, irresolute, he does not set us free.
Homilies on the Psalms, Homily 55, Psalm 145 (146) (FOTC 48)

GRACE AND PROVIDENCE—*Doctrine*

237. What could be gentler, what could be more kind, than the Lord? He is tempted by the Pharisees, their plots are wrecked, and according to the Psalmist: "The little children's arrows have become their wounds" (Psalm 64.7). Nonetheless, on account of the priesthood and the dignity of their office he exhorts the people to be subject to them and to take into consideration their teaching, but not their works.
Commentary on Matthew, Book Four (Matthew 22.41–28.20), 23.1–3 (FOTC 117)

GRACE AND PROVIDENCE—*Eternal Life*

238. Because we were mortals subject to death on account of our sin, {Jesus} deigned to die for mortals, that we might regain life through Him.
Homilies on the Psalms, Homily 29, Psalm 102 (103) (FOTC 48)

GRACE AND PROVIDENCE—*Faith*

239. The grace of the Gospel consists not in slavery but in a faith that liberates.
Commentary on Galatians, Book One (Galatians 1.1–3.9), 2.7–9 (FOTC 121)

GRACE AND PROVIDENCE—*Free Will*

240. The grace of the free will was not bestowed so as to do away with the assistance of God in every single action.
The Dialogue Against the Pelagians, Book One, paragraph 4 (FOTC 53)

GRACE AND PROVIDENCE—*Gratitude*

241. Let us, therefore, thank our leader, Jesus, for with him as leader, with him fighting for us, we are victorious.
Homilies on the Psalms, Homily 10, Psalm 76 (77) (FOTC 48)

GRACE AND PROVIDENCE—*Humility*

242. In truth, how can anything be very great that has an end?
Homilies on the Psalms, Homily 19, Psalm 89 (90) (FOTC 48)

243. Fasting is of great benefit to the Christian soul. It humbles the body and with the humiliation of the body, the soul, too, is humbled; but although the body has been reduced to submission, the soul nevertheless suffers its own passions. Now if to the flame of the soul is added the flame of the body, who is able to endure such twofold burning? Prayer frequently extinguishes the fire of the soul, and likewise does trust in the Lord.
Homilies on the Psalms, Homily 33, Psalm 106 (107) (FOTC 48)

244. Earthly creatures do not leave earth for heaven, nor heavenly beings for earth; they serve you.
Homilies on the Psalms, Homily 58, Psalm 148 (FOTC 48)

245. It is a sign of very manifest folly for man to say that he is what God is.
The Dialogue Against the Pelagians, Preface, paragraph 2 (FOTC 53)

GRACE AND PROVIDENCE—*Obedience*

246. Those who do not obey their fathers, do not obey God ... He who rejects the apostles, rejects Christ; he who rejects his father, rejects Christ who is in him.
Various Homilies, Homily 95—On Obedience (FOTC 57)

GRACE AND PROVIDENCE—*Protection*

247. In the world, a shield is one thing and a crown another, but with God, He Himself is our shield, He Himself is our crown. He protects us as if He were a shield; as God He crowns us. He is our shield; He is our crown.
Homilies on the Psalms, Homily 2, Psalm 5 (FOTC 48)

248. I have not put my trust in my sword, nor have I put my trust in my strength; but in your help I have taken refuge.
Homilies on the Psalms, Homily 3, Psalm 7 (FOTC 48)

249. When Holy Writ says sheep, it is a figure for the innocent. Sheep have nothing save a shepherd.
Homilies on the Psalms, Homily 12, Psalm 78 (79) (FOTC 48)

250. It is right for the Potter to feel pity for His works, for the Shepherd to be compassionate of His flock. We are His people, we are His creatures.
Homilies on the Psalms, Homily 17, Psalm 84 (85) (FOTC 48)

251. One who seeks refuge is looking for protection, either from the rage of fire and burning heat, or from some beast's attack, or from enemies who seek to kill him.
Homilies on the Psalms, Homily 19, Psalm 89 (90) (FOTC 48)

252. He who is fearful has a rock-fastness for his refuge; the rock, moreover, is Christ.
Homilies on the Psalms, Homily 30, Psalm 103 (104) (FOTC 48)

253. Your wandering sheep cannot be cured of its waywardness unless You carry it upon Your shoulders.
Homilies on the Psalms, Homily 54, Psalm 143 (144) (FOTC 48)

254. The just man does not fear the attack of adversaries because he has God for his helper, who surveys the universe and does not permit his poor man to be deceived by their frauds or wounded by their darts.
Homilies on the Psalms: Second Series, Homily 60, Psalm 10 (11) (FOTC 57)

255. The Lord guards the souls of his faithful ones. ... He who loves good and hates evil, what does he deserve from the Lord but His guardianship?
Homilies on the Psalms: Second Series, Homily 73, Psalm 96 (97) (FOTC 57)

256. What greater thing could be given to the faithful servant than to be with the master and to see the joy of his master?
Commentary on Matthew, Book Four (Matthew 22.41–28.20), 25.21 (FOTC 117)

257. The saints begged God to help them in their every single act, and... they had to rely on him as their helper and protector in every single deed that they performed.
The Dialogue Against the Pelagians, Book One, paragraph 5 (FOTC 53)

GRACE AND PROVIDENCE—*Redemption*

258. Let us give thanks to the omnipotent God and say: In Your human soul You had no sin; ... Help us, O Lord; just as you overpowered the devil in your human soul, vanquish the devil in ours, too, so that just as you created us a whole man, you may redeem us a whole man. You are Creator; you are Master; you are Lord; you are he who suffered for us...
Homilies on the Psalms, Homily 35, Psalm 108 (109) (FOTC 48)

259. In comparison to heaven and earth and the sea, we men in our creaturehood are as the ant or the flea. Does it stand to reason that He who created heaven and earth does not have the power to save man whom He made?
Homilies on the Psalms, Homily 55, Psalm 145 (146) (FOTC 48)

GRACE AND PROVIDENCE—*Salvation*

260. You should not inquire about the timing, when you are beholding the salvation of believers.
Commentary on Matthew, Book Two (Matthew 11.2–16.12), 11.23 (FOTC 117)

GRACE AND PROVIDENCE—*Sanctity*

261. If, therefore, earth is to be judged and not heaven, sins are not committed in heaven.
Homilies on the Psalms, Homily 14, Psalm 81 (82) (FOTC 48)

262. Whatever [blessings] God in his wisdom has conferred on the entire human race as if he were doing so on just one son, these same [blessings] he has always lavished on each one of the saints at times and places appropriate for them.
Commentary on Galatians, Book Two (Galatians 3.10–5.6), 4.8–9 (FOTC 121)

GRACE AND PROVIDENCE—*Sovereignty*

263. Does the potter not know his own pottery? He who makes another hear, will he himself be deaf? He who gave me eyes, will he himself be blind? He who is the author of my understanding, will he himself be without intelligence?
Homilies on the Psalms, Homily 22, Psalm 93 (94) (FOTC 48)

264. They do not want King Jesus; let them have King Barabbas.
Homilies on the Psalms, Homily 35, Psalm 108 (109) (FOTC 48)

265. [God's] names are as many as his kindnesses.
Homilies on the Psalms, Homily 54, Psalm 143 (144) (FOTC 48)

266. Each one is called a son of that thing whose works he carries out.
Commentary on Matthew, Book Four (Matthew 22.41–28.20), 23.15 (FOTC 117)

267. All things depend on the judgment of him who is the Creator of all things, and everything that we have is to be regarded as his gift.
The Dialogue Against the Pelagians, Book One, paragraph 2 (FOTC 53)

GRACE AND PROVIDENCE—*Temptation*

268. The devil can be a helper and an inciter of evil thoughts, but he cannot be their author. Yet he always lies in wait and kindles small sparks in our thoughts with his own tinder.
Commentary on Matthew, Book Two (Matthew 11.2–16.12), 15.19 (FOTC 117)

269. Besides our own will, we depend on the help of God in the good that we do, and on the help of the devil in the evil that we do.
The Dialogue Against the Pelagians, Book One, paragraph 2 (FOTC 53)

GRACE AND PROVIDENCE—*Trust*

270. Let us put our trust in no one save God alone. Do not let us say: if this or that should happen to me, on what would I live? I answer you: if persecution should break out, would your resources be any greater? For the Christian, there is always persecution; nakedness has always been his lot. ... You have Christ, and yet you are afraid?
Homilies on the Psalms, Homily 34, Psalm 107 (108) (FOTC 48)

Grace and Providence—*Virtue*

271. Confirm the salvation you have brought us through your Passion, and help us, for we are men, and unable to advance in virtue without your aid.
Homilies on the Psalms, Homily 7, Psalm 67 (68) (FOTC 48)

Heresy

Heresy—*Damnation*

272. The doer of evil has, indeed, killed his own soul; but the heretic—the liar—has killed as many souls as he has seduced.
Homilies on the Psalms, Homily 2, Psalm 5 (FOTC 48)

273. Every heretic is bloodthirsty, for every day he spills the blood of souls.
Homilies on the Psalms, Homily 2, Psalm 5 (FOTC 48)

Heresy—*Deceit*

274. {The heretic} is both a murderer and a practitioner of deceit. How is he deceitful? His words deliberately misrepresent the words of the Lord.
Homilies on the Psalms, Homily 2, Psalm 5 (FOTC 48)

275. The mouths of heretics are forever gaping.
Homilies on the Psalms, Homily 2, Psalm 5 (FOTC 48)

276. {Heretics} mean one thing in their heart; they promise another with their lips. They speak with piety and conceal impiety. They speak

Christ and hide the Antichrist, for they know that they will never succeed with their seduction if they disclose the Antichrist. They present light only to conceal darkness, through light they lead to darkness.
Homilies on the Psalms, Homily 2, Psalm 5 (FOTC 48)

277. Heretics change or alter their doctrine from day to day. In fact, if a theologian learned in the Scriptures contends with them, overwhelming them with proof from the Sacred Books, what do they do but straightaway look around in search of a new doctrine. They do not seek knowledge for the sake of salvation, but look around for new doctrine to vanquish the opponent.
Homilies on the Psalms, Homily 2, Psalm 5 (FOTC 48)

278. All the miserable assemblies of heretics are pits of the devil.
Homilies on the Psalms, Homily 3, Psalm 7 (FOTC 48)

279. {Heretics} do know how to speak with eloquence. They are facile with words.
Homilies on the Psalms, Homily 11, Psalm 77 (78) (FOTC 48)

280. These enemies of God's are not, therefore, from the mountain, but from the fruitless valley.
Homilies on the Psalms, Homily 15, Psalm 82 (83) (FOTC 48)

281. Your people's enemies are not of your flock or of your herd, but are stallions that rage with madness over the fillies.
Homilies on the Psalms, Homily 15, Psalm 82 (83) (FOTC 48)

282. The flying arrow of the devil, if you ask me, is the disputation of heretics... for they promise the light of knowledge, and claim that they have the light of day. They cannot deceive us, however, except by promising light. The real light they promise, however, is the fire of flaming arrows.
Homilies on the Psalms, Homily 20, Psalm 90 (91) (FOTC 48)

283. When heretics promise any pseudo mysteries, when they promise the kingdom of heaven, when they promise continence, fasts, sanctity, the renunciation of the world, they promise the noonday. But since their midday is not the light of Christ, it is not the noonday, but the noonday demon.
Homilies on the Psalms, Homily 20, Psalm 90 (91) (FOTC 48)

284. {Heretics} are skilled bowmen who, under cover of their own darkness, which they recognize as the divine mysteries concealed from them, are eager to strike at the unoffending hearts of the just.
Homilies on the Psalms: Second Series, Homily 60, Psalm 10 (11) (FOTC 57)

285. So vast is the number of heretics and so great their diversity in dogma, that, though among themselves they differ greatly in opinions and doctrines, in their hatred of us, they are of one accord. Just as Herod and Pilate, for example, who were enemies, made their peace in persecuting Christ, and were more formidable in their amity than their enmity, so the heretics, impiously at variance, league together for still greater impiety.
Homilies on the Psalms: Second Series, Homily 62, Psalm 82 (83) (FOTC 57)

286. Just as a wheel is not of itself fixed and firm, so, likewise, heretics are not firmly settled in their doctrines and opinions, but are always changing them.
Homilies on the Psalms: Second Series, Homily 62, Psalm 82 (83) (FOTC 57)

287. The teachings of heretics are the traps of death.
Homilies on the Psalms: Second Series, Homily 68, Psalm 90 (91) (FOTC 57)

288. Heretics always promise deep, dark secrets in order to ravage and tear in pieces what is true and clear.
Homilies on the Psalms: Second Series, Homily 68, Psalm 90 (91) (FOTC 57)

289. The teaching of the heretics… flies hither and thither throughout the day—throughout all God's law—in their anxious search to gather testimony against us that they may rob us of all truth by their interpretation.
Homilies on the Psalms: Second Series, Homily 68, Psalm 90 (91) (FOTC 57)

290. We, however, shall interpret the noonday devils as the heresiarchs who, while simulating angels of light, preach dogmas of darkness.
Homilies on the Psalms: Second Series, Homily 68, Psalm 90 (91) (FOTC 57)

HERESY—*Discord*

291. Heretics do not have Christ, the Truth, on their lips because they do not have Him in their heart.
Homilies on the Psalms, Homily 2, Psalm 5 (FOTC 48)

292. Heretics are unhappy men.
Homilies on the Psalms, Homily 2, Psalm 5 (FOTC 48)

293. No matter who the heretics are, they all have their superstitions.
Homilies on the Psalms, Homily 11, Psalm 77 (78) (FOTC 48)

294. {Heretics'} crop is not old but new; it is not from the old law, nor from the prophets nor apostles, but from new teachers. … Granted that many heresies are old, nevertheless, since they change daily and are discovered anew each day, they are new; even though they are old stories, because their doctrine is retold, they are new. As a matter of

fact, heretics are not content with the errors of ancient teachers; they must find new ones. ... Their ideas... are new; their words... are borrowed from worldly wisdom and well ordered; their speech is facile and elegant. ... They do not have the true Church, but only an image of the church. ... The heretics possess storehouses, for they have words hoarded for disputation. On the other hand, churchmen are undesigning; they do not anticipate their arguments. They open their mouths, and the Lord fills them just as he promised... You see, we do not have storehouses all stocked up, but our plenty abounds at that moment.
Homilies on the Psalms, Homily 54, Psalm 143 (144) (FOTC 48)

295. Heretics are never constant in their convictions, but are forever changing their opinions, shifting back and forth.
Homilies on the Psalms: Second Series, Homily 68, Psalm 90 (91) (FOTC 57)

296. To be sure, the heretics are in a much worse state than the pagans, since in the latter there is the hope of faith, in the former a battle of discord.
Commentary on Matthew, Book Two (Matthew 11.2–16.12), 12.43, 45 (FOTC 117)

Heresy—*Injustice*

297. Just think of the condition of the heretic: the Lord abhors him!
Homilies on the Psalms, Homily 2, Psalm 5 (FOTC 48)

Heresy—*Pride*

298. The praise of heretics, the balm with which they anoint the heads of men and promise them the kingdom of heaven, fattens the head with pride.
Homilies on the Psalms, Homily 51, Psalm 140 (141) (FOTC 48)

Heresy—*Righteousness*

299. O you who glory in abstinence, glory in your gatherings and do not defend heresies to your own satisfaction.
Homilies on the Psalms, Homily 7, Psalm 67 (68) (FOTC 48)

300. Jesus' outcry is in the narrow way, not in the avenues of the heretics.
Homilies on the Psalms, Homily 54, Psalm 143 (144) (FOTC 48)

Heresy—*Sovereignty*

301. Let {heretics} fall by their own countless contrivances and let them have but one recourse, You, my God.
Homilies on the Psalms, Homily 2, Psalm 5 (FOTC 48)

302. The heretics have forgotten their Father and his wonderful deeds in the land of Egypt; in the darkness of this world, have forgotten how by his deliverance they were reborn in the Church.
Homilies on the Psalms, Homily 11, Psalm 77 (78) (FOTC 48)

303. They who trust in their own wisdom and not in the glory of God rot on the ground like dung.
Homilies on the Psalms, Homily 15, Psalm 82 (83) (FOTC 48)

Heresy—*Temptation*

304. The devil always has his bow ready and he is ever alert to shoot his arrows and strike us down.
Homilies on the Psalms, Homily 3, Psalm 7 (FOTC 48)

305. Just as the Lord has his chosen saints, so does the devil have his elect. Think of the chief heretics and you will have no doubt about his chosen band.
Homilies on the Psalms, Homily 51, Psalm 140 (141) (FOTC 48)

HERESY—*Vice*

306. Heretics or demons are forever setting traps for us. Vice is certainly the next door neighbor to virtue.
Homilies on the Psalms, Homily 51, Psalm 140 (141) (FOTC 48)

HERESY—*Vigilance*

307. Now the heretics speak and the churchmen hold their peace; they raise an uproar, but we keep silence; they blaspheme, and we are not enraged. ... Their speech is not ordered and constructive, but only a noise, confused and disruptive.
Homilies on the Psalms: Second Series, Homily 62, Psalm 82 (83) (FOTC 57)

308. Those who are put in charge of the Church must not fall asleep. Otherwise, while they are showing such negligence, the enemy man will introduce the sowing of weeds, that is, the dogmas of the heretics.
Commentary on Matthew, Book Two (Matthew 11.2–16.12), 13.37 (FOTC 117)

309. Just as tombs are smoothed over on the outside with chalk, adorned with marble, and distinguished with gold and colors, but inside they are full of dead man's bones, so also are bad teachers. They teach one thing and do something else. They may show purity in the quality of their clothing and in the humility of their words, but inwardly they are full of all filth, avarice, and lust.
Commentary on Matthew, Book Four (Matthew 22.41–28.20), 23.27 (FOTC 117)

310. I am of the opinion that all heresiarchs are antichrists and teach things in the name of Christ that are contrary to Christ. It is not surprising that we see some seduced by them, since the Lord said: "And they will seduce many."
Commentary on Matthew, Book Four (Matthew 22.41–28.20), 24.5 (FOTC 117)

311. The faith of the church, then, is trapped among formidable shipwrecks of false teaching.
Commentary on Galatians, Book One (Galatians 1.1–3.9), 1.1 (FOTC 121)

312. Heretical plagues do not possess the Gospel of God because they do not have the Holy Spirit, and without the Spirit the Gospel that is taught ceases to be divine.
Commentary on Galatians, Book One (Galatians 1.1–3.9), 1.11–12 (FOTC 121)

313. The truth by its nature cannot be anything but truth. Everyone who interprets the Gospel in a spirit or mentality at odds with what is written in Scripture causes a disturbance to believers and undermines the Gospel of Christ, causing what is in front to appear behind, and vice versa.
Commentary on Galatians, Book One (Galatians 1.1–3.9), 1.6–7 (FOTC 121)

Humility

HUMILITY—*Christ*

314. See how Christ esteems humility. Christ, the Son of God, is not recognized in the Temple, but he is proclaimed in the desert. The humble Christ loves the humble.
Various Homilies: Second Series, Homily 87—On the Gospel of John 1.1–14 (FOTC 57)

315. The Lord descends to the humble places and to the fields, in order to overcome the devil by humility.
Commentary on Matthew, Book One (Matthew 1.1–10.42), 4.8 (FOTC 117)

316. He who becomes the kind of person who imitates the humility and innocence of Christ, in him Christ is received.
Commentary on Matthew, Book Three (Matthew 16.13–22.40), 18.5 (FOTC 117)

HUMILITY—*Envy*

317. The person who imitates the riches, power, and eminence of someone else emulates not what is good but what ought to be shunned.
Commentary on Galatians, Book Two (Galatians 3.10–5.6), 4.17–18 (FOTC 121)

HUMILITY—*Mercy*

318. If you are a sinner, do not despair of pardon; the Lord is merciful. If you are proud and presume upon the mercy of God, be careful; he is also just.
Homilies on the Psalms, Homily 38, Psalm 111 (112) (FOTC 48)

HUMILITY—*Obedience*

319. Where there is obedience, there is humility.
Homilies on the Gospel of Saint Mark on Various Topics, Homily 82 (VIII)—On Mark 11.11–14 (FOTC 57)

320. The man who does not obey is not motivated from holiness, but from pride, for it goes without saying that he who does not obey thinks himself better than the one to whom he refuses submission.
Various Homilies, Homily 95—On Obedience (FOTC 57)

Humility—*Penance*

321. He who desires to attain the kingdom of heaven, let him pray night and day; let him keep watch; let him fast; let him make his bed on rushes, not on down and silk. Penitence has no fellowship with soft luxuries.
Homilies on the Psalms, Homily 22, Psalm 93 (94) (FOTC 48)

Humility—*Pride*

322. The devil is the prince of the proud.
Homilies on the Psalms: Second Series, Homily 71, Psalm 93 (94) (FOTC 57)

323. All other failings deserve the mercy of the Lord because, in humility, they are submitted to the tribunal of God; pride alone, because it honors itself beyond its power, resists God.
Homilies on the Psalms: Second Series, Homily 71, Psalm 93 (94) (FOTC 57)

324. The sinner who supplicates God merits pardon, but the man who vaunts himself in wickedness is proud, and pride makes God an enemy.
Homilies on the Psalms: Second Series, Homily 71, Psalm 93 (94) (FOTC 57)

325. Pride never brings salvation, but humility does.
Various Homilies, Homily 88—On the Nativity of the Lord (FOTC 57)

326. We are mild about an injury to God, but annoyed to the point of hatred about insults to ourselves!
Commentary on Matthew, Book Three (Matthew 16.13–22.40), 18.15–17 (FOTC 117)

327. If almsgiving is done for the purpose of obtaining praise, it is empty glory, and the same goes for prolonged prayer and the pallor caused by fasting. These words are not mine but the Savior's, who thunderously proclaims them in the Gospel (cf. Matthew 6.1–6, 16–18). Chastity in marriage, widowhood, and virginity also often seek human applause.... If we undergo martyrdom with the intention of being marveled at and praised by our brothers, then blood has been shed in vain. *Commentary on Galatians*, Book Three (Galatians 5.7–6.18), 5.26 (FOTC 121)

HUMILITY—*Providence*

328. It is to be observed that God is opening his eyes in bringing manifest justice to the support of the humble man, for even if he is alone and poor, God's solicitous glance is always upon him. *Homilies on the Psalms: Second Series*, Homily 60, Psalm 10 (11) (FOTC 57)

329. The humble man, who sacrifices all he has for the sake of Christ, is a valley and a field that is not barren, but fruitful. *Homilies on the Psalms: Second Series*, Homily 62, Psalm 82 (83) (FOTC 57)

330. Acknowledgement of helplessness promptly wins the help of God, for he is as much appeased by humility as he is offended by pride. *Homilies on the Psalms: Second Series*, Homily 71, Psalm 93 (94) (FOTC 57)

HUMILITY—*Purity*

331. Nothing so pleases God as simplicity and purity of heart. The Holy Spirit, in fact, takes great pleasure in no other bird than the

dove because of its simplicity, and no other quadruped than the sheep because of its gentleness.
Homilies on the Psalms, Homily 27, Psalm 100 (101) (FOTC 48)

332. Praise that is pure and simple is not so highly concerned about its acceptance on the part of the listeners.
The Apology Against the Books of Rufinus, Book One, paragraph 1 (FOTC 53)

HUMILITY—*Repentance*

333. When I ponder over my sins, I do not dare raise my eyes to heaven.
Homilies on the Psalms, Homily 10, Psalm 76 (77) (FOTC 48)

334. There is this about pride: to itself, it always passes for wisdom. … Pride is contrary to God because it does not submit to him; hence, the proud man considers himself just. He does not repent of his evil deeds, but glories in his sham good works.
Various Homilies, Homily 95—On Obedience (FOTC 57)

HUMILITY—*Righteousness*

335. We must be careful, therefore, not to permit ourselves from custom to esteem lightly the goodness of our Lord.
Homilies on the Psalms, Homily 46, Psalm 133 (134) (FOTC 48)

HUMILITY—*Service*

336. It is a noble tribute, indeed, to be called men of God, or servants of God. When anyone is so designated, it is a sign, not of his lowliness, but of his dignity, for it is not the condition of servitude that is emphasized, but the distinction of serving well.

Homilies on the Psalms: Second Series, Homily 67, Psalm 89 (90) (FOTC 57)

Humility—*Sin*

337. It is precisely because we had been so elevated that we are said to have fallen.
Homilies on the Psalms, Homily 14, Psalm 81 (82) (FOTC 48)

Humility—*Sovereignty*

338. Let no one, therefore, say: I am a bishop; I am a priest, or a deacon, or a monk; I am a prince in this world. God is powerful enough to destroy the spirit of princes. Again, that you may be sure that God curbs the spirit of pride, recall how the good spirit of God departed from Saul and an evil spirit troubled him.
Homilies on the Psalms, Homily 9, Psalm 75 (76) (FOTC 48)

339. No matter how high anyone may exalt himself, we have God who is Lord over all.
Homilies on the Psalms, Homily 15, Psalm 82 (83) (FOTC 48)

Humility—*Virtue*

340. One comes to the summit of virtue not by power, but by humility.
Commentary on Matthew, Book Three (Matthew 16.13–22.40), 20.25 (FOTC 117)

Humility—*Weakness*

341. If God has made all things, and has made them all for the needs of man, why did he have to make bugs and fleas? I shall make my

answer to you brief and to the point: in order to expose your frailty, O man. You, who set your thoughts in heaven, look down; you are being bitten by a bug and you are trembling.
Homilies on the Psalms, Homily 21, Psalm 91 (92) (FOTC 48)

342. Human weakness is not patient in bearing the sight of greater glory.
Commentary on Matthew, Book Three (Matthew 16.13–22.40), 17.6 (FOTC 117)

HUMILITY—*Worldliness*

343. Unless the earth tremble and withdraw from its worldly pursuits, the Lord will not reign among the nations.
Homilies on the Psalms, Homily 23, Psalm 95 (96) (FOTC 48)

HUMILITY—*Worship*

344. Happy that servant through whom the master receives honor and glory.
Homilies on the Psalms, Homily 23, Psalm 95 (96) (FOTC 48)

The Incarnation

THE INCARNATION—*Divine Revelation*

345. What is the presence of God if not Christ?
Homilies on the Psalms, Homily 50, Psalm 139 (140) (FOTC 48)

346. It is disgraceful for us to be indolent in the presence of Jesus.
Homilies on the Gospel of Saint Mark on Various Topics, Homily 76 (II)—On Mark 1.13–31 (FOTC 57)

347. Wherever {Jesus} wills, there He is; wherever He is, He is there whole and entire. Wherever He is and wherever you are, you who are seeking Him are in Him whom you seek.
Various Homilies, Homily 87—On the Gospel of John 1.1–14 (FOTC 57)

348. Because we could not see [the Lord] as long as he was the Word, let us see his flesh because it is flesh; let us see how the Word was made flesh.
Various Homilies, Homily 88—On the Nativity of the Lord (FOTC 57)

349. As long as the Son of God was in heaven, he was not adored; he descends to earth and is adored. He had beneath him the sun, the moon, the angels, and he was not adored; on earth, he is born perfect man, a whole man, to heal the whole world.
Various Homilies, Homily 88—On the Nativity of the Lord (FOTC 57)

350. But as for what it says: "He was transfigured before them," let no one think that he has lost his original form and appearance, or that he lost the reality of his body and took up either a spiritual or an airy body. ... When the splendor of the face is shown and the brilliance of the clothing is described, it is not that the substance is removed, but the glory is changed.
Commentary on Matthew, Book Three (Matthew 16.13–22.40), 17.2 (FOTC 117)

THE INCARNATION—*Holiness*

351. Holiness personified offered itself to erase wickedness; and strength, feebleness.
Commentary on Galatians, Book One (Galatians 1.1–3.9), 1.4–5 (FOTC 121)

THE INCARNATION—*Humility*

352. [The Lord] found no room in the Holy of Holies that shone with gold, precious stones, pure silk, and silver. He is not born in the midst of gold and riches, but in the midst of dung, in a stable (wherever there is a stable, there is also dung) where our sins were more filthy than the dung. He is born on a dunghill in order to lift up those who come from it; "from the dunghill he lifts up the poor" (Psalm 112.7).
Various Homilies, Homily 88—On the Nativity of the Lord (FOTC 57)

353. I wonder at the Lord, the Creator of the universe, who is born, not surrounded by gold and silver, but by mud and clay.
Various Homilies, Homily 88—On the Nativity of the Lord (FOTC 57)

THE INCARNATION—*The Hypostatic Union*

354. If {the Church} confesses that Christ is [only] man, then Ebion and Photinus gain ground. If it contends that he is [only] God, then Mani, Marcion, and the author of the new teaching all bubble up to the surface. Let each and every one of them hear that Christ is both God and man—not that one is God, and the other man, but rather, that he who is God from all eternity deigned to become man in order to save us.
Commentary on Galatians, Book One (Galatians 1.1–3.9), 1.1 (FOTC 121)

355. [Christ] is the Son of man only insofar as he is the Son of God.
The Dialogue Against the Pelagians, Book One, paragraph 20 (FOTC 53)

THE INCARNATION—*The Paschal Mystery*

356. These are the mighty deeds, these are the wonders of God: that God became man, was hidden in the womb of a virgin; was born and

lay in a manger; that He who healed the wounds of men was wounded by them, struck with blows, crucified; that He who is immortal suffered death and bore patiently so much unjust punishment, lest men be unable to endure retribution for their sins.
Homilies on the Psalms: Second Series, Homily 66, Psalm 88 (89) (FOTC 57)

357. Everything that Jesus did points to our salvation.
Homilies on the Gospel of Saint Mark on Various Topics, Homily 81 (VII)—On Mark 11.1–10 (FOTC 57)

358. If Israel had believed, our Lord would not have been crucified. If our Lord had not been crucified, the multitude of Gentiles would not have been saved.
Homilies on the Gospel of Saint Mark on Various Topics, Homily 82 (VIII)—On Mark 11.11–14 (FOTC 57)

359. We reach the mystery of the cross through the perfect Word that is Christ.
Homilies on the Gospel of Saint Mark on Various Topics, Homily 84 (X)—On Mark 13.32–33 and 14.3–6 (FOTC 57)

360. Let them blush who think that the Savior feared death and that it was out of dread of suffering that he said: "Father, if it is possible, let this cup pass from me" (Matthew 26.39).
Commentary on Matthew, Book Four (Matthew 22.41–28.20), 26.1–2 (FOTC 117)

THE INCARNATION—*Redemption*

361. Let us... acknowledge and give thanks that {Jesus} had a true body and a true soul, for if the Lord did not assume human nature in its totality, then He did not redeem mankind. If He assumed the body only, but not the soul, He saved the body, but not the soul. But

we want our soul to be saved far more than our body; hence, the Lord assumed both body and soul to redeem both body and soul, to redeem the whole man just as He made him.
Homilies on the Psalms, Homily 35, Psalm 108 (109) (FOTC 48)

362. Let us continue our adoration of {the Babe} today. Let us pick Him up in our arms and adore Him as the Son of God. Mighty God who for so long a time thundered in heaven and did not redeem man, cries and as a babe redeems him.
Various Homilies, Homily 88—On the Nativity of the Lord (FOTC 57)

363. Just as Christ was put under the Law to redeem those under the Law, so also did he want to be born of a woman for the sake of those who had also been born of a woman.
Commentary on Galatians, Book Two (Galatians 3.10–5.6), 4.4–5 (FOTC 121)

The Incarnation—*Sacred Scripture*

364. Wisdom itself, in assuming a human body, in dying and rising from the dead, manifests that he was not without the Father's counsel, but totally in accord with Scripture.
Homilies on the Psalms: Second Series, Homily 61, Psalm 15 (16) (FOTC 57)

365. He was speaking himself in person who previously had spoken by the prophets.
Homilies on the Gospel of Saint Mark on Various Topics, Homily 76 (II)—On Mark 1.13–31 (FOTC 57)

366. They who went before and they who followed, cry out aloud in one voice. Who are they who go before? Patriarchs and prophets.

Who follow? Apostles and Gentiles. In those who precede and in those who follow, however, it is Christ who speaks; Him they are praising; Him they acclaim with one harmonious voice.
Homilies on the Gospel of Saint Mark on Various Topics, Homily 81 (VII)—On Mark 11.1–10 (FOTC 57)

THE INCARNATION—*Sovereignty*

367. Not that I may divide Christ; not that there is one Christ, another Jesus, another Son of God; but that the One and the Same is distinguished by us according to the divisions of time.
Homilies on the Gospel of Saint Mark on Various Topics, Homily 75 (I)—On the Beginning of the Gospel of Saint Mark (1.1–12) (FOTC 57)

THE INCARNATION—*Truth*

368. The sages of Greece, the barbarian peoples, the Romans—the cesspool of all superstition—worship the sun, moon, seas, and the gods of the forests and mountains. When Christ came, we were freed from such superstitions.
Commentary on Galatians, Book Two (Galatians 3.10–5.6), 4.3 (FOTC 121)

THE INCARNATION—*Vigilance*

369. When… {the Lord} assumed a human body, he saw the opposing power; he saw, too, the army of the devil drawn up in wedge formation against him.
Homilies on the Psalms: Second Series, Homily 61, Psalm 15 (16) (FOTC 57)

Judgment

JUDGMENT—*Condemnation*

370. No one descends into hell in triumph save you alone, Lord.
Homilies on the Psalms, Homily 34, Psalm 107 (108) (FOTC 48)

JUDGMENT—*Eternity*

371. We do not believe in this life, but in the future life; nor do we believe in him in order to escape burning here, but in order to escape passing from this fire into another fire.
Homilies on the Psalms, Homily 55, Psalm 145 (146) (FOTC 48)

372. After the day of judgment, the opportunity for good works and for justice will disappear.
Commentary on Matthew, Book Four (Matthew 22.41–28.20), 25.10 (FOTC 117)

373. While we are in the present age, we are able to be helped by one another's prayers and counsel. When we come before the judgment seat of Christ, however, neither Job nor Daniel nor Noah will be able to intercede on behalf of anyone, but each person will carry his own burden.
Commentary on Galatians, Book Three (Galatians 5.7–6.18), 6.5 (FOTC 121)

374. Just as there is a time for sowing and a time for harvesting, so also in the present life the sowing concerns works which are sown in the Spirit or in the flesh, while the harvest is the future judgment of works.
Commentary on Galatians, Book Three (Galatians 5.7–6.18), 6.9 (FOTC 121)

JUDGMENT—*Forgiveness*

375. It is an alarming sentence of judgment, if God's verdict is changed and altered on the basis of our attitude of mind. If we do not forgive our brothers trivial things, God will not forgive us great things.
Commentary on Matthew, Book Three (Matthew 16.13–22.40), 18.25 (FOTC 117)

JUDGMENT—*Holiness*

376. Every sinner fears the judgment of God; he does not want to know the judge, he wants to meet with mercy. The man of holiness, however, both heeds God and glorifies him in his body; he does not fear the judge, he loves him.
Homilies on the Psalms, Homily 26, Psalm 98 (99) (FOTC 48)

JUDGMENT—*Purgatory*

377. Whatever is above is gold; whatever is below is ready for the purgatory of Gehenna.
Homilies on the Psalms, Homily 56, Psalm 146 (147A) (FOTC 48)

378. In baptism, our guilt is taken away; in repentance, however, sins that have been committed are "covered"; they are not wiped out, but are forgiven.
Homilies on the Psalms: Second Series, Homily 64, Psalm 84 (85) (FOTC 57)

379. Let us beg the Apostles to intercede for us with Jesus, that he may come to us and touch our hand… Excellent physician, and truly the chief physician!
Homilies on the Gospel of Saint Mark on Various Topics, Homily 76 (II)—On Mark 1.13–31 (FOTC 57)

380. You will not come out from prison until you pay in full for even the least sins.
Commentary on Matthew, Book One (Matthew 1.1–10.42), 5.25–5.26 (FOTC 117)

JUDGMENT—*Purity*

381. It pertains to one with great confidence and a pure conscience to ask for the kingdom of God without fearing the judgment.
Commentary on Matthew, Book One (Matthew 1.1–10.42), 6.10 (FOTC 117)

JUDGMENT—*Sin*

382. Those who refuse to know the Father, let them experience the Judge.
Homilies on the Psalms, Homily 2, Psalm 5 (FOTC 48)

383. The wicked, confirmed in malice and iniquity and rebelling against the Lord with all their soul, have no chance before God's judgment; but other men who are sinners and sometimes confused with the malicious do have a chance because of their wrongdoing is of a lesser degree.
Homilies on the Psalms: Second Series, Homily 60, Psalm 10 (11) (FOTC 57)

384. If each person will render an account on the day of judgment for his words, how much more are you going to render an account for your false charges!
Commentary on Matthew, Book Two (Matthew 11.2–16.12), 12.36 (FOTC 117)

385. No man goes before the judgment of God without trepidation, being conscious of his sins.
The Dialogue Against the Pelagians, Book Two, paragraph 22 (FOTC 53)

JUDGMENT—*Temperance*

386. You must be judges, not wolves.
Homilies on the Psalms, Homily 14, Psalm 81 (82) (FOTC 48)

JUDGMENT—*Testimony*

387. For at that time {of judgment}, there will be no room for impudence, nor the capability of denying, since all the angels and the world itself will be a witness against sinners.
Commentary on Matthew, Book Three (Matthew 16.13–22.40), 22.11–12 (FOTC 117)

JUDGMENT—*Truth*

388. Rise, O you, who are the true Judge.
Homilies on the Psalms, Homily 14, Psalm 81 (82) (FOTC 48)

JUDGMENT—*Vanity*

389. The Lord knows the thoughts of men, and that they are vain. So long as we are men, our thoughts are vain.
Homilies on the Psalms: Second Series, Homily 71, Psalm 93 (94) (FOTC 57)

JUDGMENT—*Wisdom*

390. The patience of the Lord they took for lack of knowledge.
Homilies on the Psalms: Second Series, Homily 71, Psalm 93 (94) (FOTC 57)

Justice

JUSTICE—*Eternal Life*

391. Those universal rewards the just man receives, the wicked man will not receive.
Homilies on the Psalms, Homily 1, Psalm 1 (FOTC 48)

392. Indeed, do I long to enter your house, and I desire to enter it by way of justice. Because my enemies are continually besetting my path with snares and setting traps for me all along the way—while my one longing is to enter your house—I am beseeching you to keep my feet firm in your path to the very end. It is mine to set my feet in your way; it is yours to direct my steps.
Homilies on the Psalms, Homily 2, Psalm 5 (FOTC 48)

393. The man who loves justice loves his own soul.
Homilies on the Psalms: Second Series, Homily 60, Psalm 10 (11) (FOTC 57)

JUSTICE—*Eternity*

394. As the just man is compared to the tree, the wicked man is compared to dust.
Homilies on the Psalms, Homily 1, Psalm 1 (FOTC 48)

395. The Lord is not judge now, but will be later. If he were judge now, sinners would not be arrogant and gain the wealth of the world. Is it a scandal to you that the just are in exile and sinners persecute them? Does it scandalize you that wickedness reigns in the world?
Homilies on the Psalms, Homily 8, Psalm 74 (75) (FOTC 48)

396. The time for judgment has been set aside. The present world is not the time of judgment, but of contest.
Homilies on the Psalms, Homily 8, Psalm 74 (75) (FOTC 48)

JUSTICE—*Hope*

397. Even if we arise in the nighttime, we are blessing God in light. For the Christian, it is never night; for the Christian, the sun of justice is ever rising.
Homilies on the Psalms, Homily 34, Psalm 107 (108) (FOTC 48)

JUSTICE—*Humanity*

398. We are all born equal, emperors and paupers; and we die as equals. Our humanity is of one quality.
Homilies on the Psalms, Homily 14, Psalm 81 (82) (FOTC 48)

JUSTICE—*Repentance*

399. If the sun of iniquity does not set for us, our Sun of justice cannot rise, whose health is in his wings.
Homilies on the Psalms, Homily 7, Psalm 67 (68) (FOTC 48)

400. It is not enough to love justice, but you must hate wickedness.
Homilies on the Psalms, Homily 45, Psalm 132 (133) (FOTC 48)

401. It does not suffice for us to want justice, if we do not experience a hunger for justice. Thus from this example we should understand that we are never sufficiently just, but it is always necessary to hunger for works of justice.
Commentary on Matthew, Book One (Matthew 1.1–10.42), 5.6 (FOTC 117)

JUSTICE—*Salvation*

402. The Lord does not know the sinner, but the just man he does know.
Homilies on the Psalms, Homily 1, Psalm 1 (FOTC 48)

JUSTICE—*Sin*

403. They who do not walk to God in justice are given over to the devil.
Homilies on the Psalms, Homily 34, Psalm 107 (108) (FOTC 48)

404. When we perform deeds of justice, we are alive; when we sin, we cease to be.
Homilies on the Psalms, Homily 55, Psalm 145 (146) (FOTC 48)

405. Let not sin contract us, but justice expand us.
Homilies on the Psalms, Homily 59, Psalm 149 (FOTC 48)

JUSTICE—*Sovereignty*

406. May we not experience him as Judge, but know him as Father.
Homilies on the Psalms, Homily 6, Psalm 66 (67) (FOTC 48)

407. [The Savior] is, indeed, Justice.
Homilies on the Psalms: Second Series, Homily 60, Psalm 10 (11) (FOTC 57)

Mercy and Compassion

MERCY AND COMPASSION—*Charity*

408. Does it deserve the name of humanity, or of mercy, to scoff at the misfortunes of others, and display before the public the wounds of others?
The Apology Against the Books of Rufinus, Book Three, paragraph 17 (FOTC 53)

MERCY AND COMPASSION—*Honesty*

409. We are just when we acknowledge that we are sinners, and our justice depends not on our own personal merit, but rather on the mercy of God.
The Dialogue Against the Pelagians, Book One, paragraph 13 (FOTC 53)

MERCY AND COMPASSION—*Hope*

410. Wherever there is the mercy of the Lord, there is light, there is dawn, there is the hour when the sun rises, and the blind shades of night vanish.
Homilies on the Psalms: Second Series, Homily 69, Psalm 91 (92) (FOTC 57)

MERCY AND COMPASSION—*Humility*

411. Let sinners who are despairing of their salvation, who are humble and broken down over their sins, hear the song of mercy; let the

arrogant who say: "The Lord is merciful, let us sin, he will pardon us," hear the song of justice.
Homilies on the Psalms, Homily 27, Psalm 100 (101) (FOTC 48)

MERCY AND COMPASSION—*Joy*

412. Because I have obtained mercy forever, I must sing forever, for the cause of my praise is eternal. He who sings sends away grief, sends away fear, and rises to joy, for he has obtained mercy.
Homilies on the Psalms: Second Series, Homily 66, Psalm 88 (89) (FOTC 57)

MERCY AND COMPASSION—*Kindness*

413. No matter how long he restrains his compassionate mercy, nevertheless, his kindness will always triumph.
Homilies on the Psalms, Homily 10, Psalm 76 (77) (FOTC 48)

414. To be compassionately kind to all his works, he looked down from heaven.
Homilies on the Psalms, Homily 17, Psalm 84 (85) (FOTC 48)

415. Are we not able to proclaim the kindness of God at noon?
Homilies on the Psalms, Homily 21, Psalm 91 (92) (FOTC 48)

416. Because we are little and lowly and unable to lift ourselves up to him, the Lord stoops down to us, and in his compassionate kindness, deigns to hear us.
Homilies on the Psalms, Homily 39, Psalm 114 (116A) (FOTC 48)

MERCY AND COMPASSION—*The Law*

417. [Jesus has] not come to make void the commandments of mercy that the Law had established, but to build upon their foundation.

Homilies on the Psalms: Second Series, Homily 66, Psalm 88 (89) (FOTC 57)

MERCY AND COMPASSION—*Patience*

418. Human impatience does not want God to have patience. Creatures truly pitiable are we who would have God patient with us but impatient with our enemies. When we commit sin, we beg God to be patient with us; yet, when somebody wrongs us, we do not expect God to be patient with him.
Homilies on the Psalms, Homily 22, Psalm 93 (94) (FOTC 48)

MERCY AND COMPASSION—*Redemption*

419. We have stressed the mercy of the Lord because His whole purpose in coming was to redeem mankind.
Homilies on the Psalms, Homily 17, Psalm 84 (85) (FOTC 48)

MERCY AND COMPASSION—*Repentance*

420. A loud cry is all the more necessary when the troubled heart is far away. This is what he is saying: because of my sins I am far away from you, and so I must cry out loud that in your gracious mercy, you may hear me.
Homilies on the Psalms, Homily 10, Psalm 76 (77) (FOTC 48)

421. It is not possible for us to confess to the Lord and obtain his mercy unless a clear light has begun to enlighten our heart. Unless the shades of night have withdrawn and dawn has arrived, we cannot attain the compassionate mercy of God. Then, in truth, do you proclaim at dawn the kindness of God, when the sun of justice has risen in your heart.
Homilies on the Psalms, Homily 21, Psalm 91 (92) (FOTC 48)

422. Let the man who repents have confidence, therefore, because the time of salvation is at hand; merciful and compassionate is the Lord.
Homilies on the Psalms, Homily 28, Psalm 101 (102) (FOTC 48)

MERCY AND COMPASSION—*Salvation*

423. You the Savior, you the Christ, and we the Christians: have mercy upon us for your name's sake.
Homilies on the Psalms, Homily 12, Psalm 78 (79) (FOTC 48)

424. The Savior's descent is the work of God's mercy. He would not have come as a Physician if most men were not sick. Because so many were sick, he came as Physician; because we were in need of compassion, he came as Savior.
Homilies on the Psalms, Homily 17, Psalm 84 (85) (FOTC 48)

MERCY AND COMPASSION—*Sovereignty*

425. God is compassionate, whereas every man is cruel.
Homilies on the Psalms, Homily 14, Psalm 81 (82) (FOTC 48)

MERCY AND COMPASSION—*Truth*

426. {God} is, indeed, merciful, but he is [also] true. When you hear he is merciful, you must not be indifferent to the "and true" that follows. On the other hand, when you shall hear that God is truth, do not despair; do not think that God is only severe, for mercy tempers truth… He has tempered in due proportion truth with mercy and mercy with truth.
Homilies on the Psalms: Second Series, Homily 63, Psalm 83 (84) (FOTC 57)

427. Indeed, at first, when I was a sinner, I did not dare to approach truth; but when I obtained mercy, then, fearlessly, with a brave heart, I proclaimed it.
Homilies on the Psalms: Second Series, Homily 66, Psalm 88 (89) (FOTC 57)

Peace

PEACE—*Charity*

428. We have left mothers, fathers, brothers, sisters; we have given up wives and children; we have given up our countries; we have left our homes; we have left behind nurseries in which we were born and reared; we have left servants with whom we grew up to manhood; we have come into a monastery; all these things we have given up in order that in the monastery, we quarrel over a reed pen!
Homilies on the Psalms, Homily 41, Psalm 119 (120) (FOTC 48)

PEACE—*Christ*

429. Let us also say to our own soul: Return to your tranquility. Our tranquility is Christ our God. If ever we are in great straits, and our thoughts are ready to capitulate to sin, let us cry out: Return, O my soul, to your tranquility. ... My feet were saved from stumbling. Why? Because my soul returned to its tranquility.
Homilies on the Psalms, Homily 39, Psalm 114 (116A) (FOTC 48)

430. Peace is the might of Christians... Blessed the peacemakers, not only those who restore peace among the quarrelsome, but those who establish peace in themselves. Blessed the peacemakers. If others engage in strife, and I intercede and bring peace to them, yet do not

have peace in my heart, what benefit to me that they are at peace? ...
Blessed the peacemakers who speak peace to those who hate peace.
Blessed the peacemakers. Christ is peace. Since Solomon represents
Christ, and Solomon means peaceful, Christ our Lord is peace. ... Let
us guard carefully the gift Christ has given us; let us preserve peace, and
it will preserve us in Christ Jesus, to whom be glory forever and ever.
Homilies on the Psalms, Homily 41, Psalm 119 (120) (FOTC 48)

431. Whoever has Christ within him, has peace within him.
Homilies on the Psalms, Homily 42, Psalm 127 (128) (FOTC 48)

432. Let false peace not destroy what war has spared. I do not want
to learn perfidy through fear, when Christ has left the true faith up
to my own will.
The Dialogue Against the Pelagians, Preface, paragraph 2 (FOTC 53)

Peace—*Conversion*

433. What use is it when others are pacified through you, if within
your own heart there are wars of vices going on?
Commentary on Matthew, Book One (Matthew 1.1–10.42), 5.9
(FOTC 117)

434. We should not suppose that peace is limited to not quarreling
with others. Rather, the peace of Christ (that is, our inheritance) is
with us when the mind is at peace and undisturbed by the passions.
Commentary on Galatians, Book Three (Galatians 5.7–6.18), 5.22–23
(FOTC 121)

Peace—*The Holy Spirit*

435. When we give way to anger, yield to detraction, surrender to
a sadness that leads to death, entertain thoughts of the flesh, do we

think that the Holy Spirit is abiding in us? Do we suppose that we may hate a brother with the Holy Spirit dwelling in us? That we may call to mind and dwell upon anything evil? On the other hand, when our thoughts are good thoughts, let us realize that the Holy Spirit is dwelling in us.
Homilies on the Gospel of Saint Mark on Various Topics, Homily 75 (I)—On the Beginning of the Gospel of Saint Mark (1.1–12) (FOTC 57)

436. The Holy Spirit does not will to dwell where there are confusion, crowds, quarrels, and dissensions.
Homilies on the Gospel of Saint Mark on Various Topics, Homily 75 (I)—On the Beginning of the Gospel of Saint Mark (1.1–12) (FOTC 57)

PEACE—*Hope*

437. God cannot speak peace to his people except to those who hope in him with all their heart.
Homilies on the Psalms, Homily 17, Psalm 84 (85) (FOTC 48)

PEACE—*Justice*

438. The Lord always shatters the shield, the sword, and the weapons of war.
Homilies on the Psalms, Homily 9, Psalm 75 (76) (FOTC 48)

PEACE—*Kindness*

439. Kindness equates to peace, truth to justice. Whatever pertains to peace belongs, likewise, to kindness; whatever refers to truth applies also to justice.
Homilies on the Psalms, Homily 17, Psalm 84 (85) (FOTC 48)

PEACE—*Self-Control*

440. I am upset because I am human; I control my tongue because I am a Christian. Anger surges up in my heart, but I do not give vent to it.
Homilies on the Psalms, Homily 10, Psalm 76 (77) (FOTC 48)

441. It is a mark of great virtue and strength to rise above affliction and control anger... Are you angry? You are a man. Anger finds no lodging in you? You are a Christian.
Homilies on the Psalms, Homily 35, Psalm 108 (109) (FOTC 48)

PEACE—*Sovereignty*

442. There is no tent of the Lord except where there is peace. Where there is strife and discord, God is not there as a Protector. ... The abode of God is only in a peaceful soul; therefore, let the soul that is without peace know that it is not the dwelling place of God. ... Peace is our legacy from the Savior.
Homilies on the Psalms, Homily 9, Psalm 75 (76) (FOTC 48)

PEACE—*Truth*

443. We must try as best we can not to have any enemy, but to keep the peace with everyone. If, by speaking the truth, we make enemies out of some, we are not so much their enemies as they are the enemies of the truth.
Commentary on Galatians, Book Three (Galatians 5.7–6.18), 5.19–21 (FOTC 121)

PEACE—*Wisdom*

444. Where there is strife, there is sin; but where there is discussion, there is conscientious desire for knowledge.

Homilies on the Psalms: Second Series, Homily 69, Psalm 91 (92) (FOTC 57)

Persecution and Martyrdom

PERSECUTION AND MARTYRDOM—*The Apostles*

445. All of us, if only we deserve to be, are the sons of martyrs.
Homilies on the Psalms, Homily 12, Psalm 78 (79) (FOTC 48)

446. Happy, indeed, is our victory consecrated in the blood of the Apostles. By their blood alone our faith is confirmed.
Homilies on the Psalms, Homily 14, Psalm 81 (82) (FOTC 48)

PERSECUTION AND MARTYRDOM—*Baptism*

447. The martyr, even though he has sinned after baptism, is cleansed by the second baptism of martyrdom, and goes to the Lord in utmost confidence.
Homilies on the Psalms, Homily 40, Psalm 115 (116B) (FOTC 48)

PERSECUTION AND MARTYRDOM—*Christ*

448. Martyrdom is a grand thing. Why? Because the martyr gives back to the Lord what he received from him. Christ suffered for him, and he suffers for the name of Christ. We said that the martyr has nothing else to give to the Lord, and that the Lord reckons it as equality, because he knows that his servant has nothing else to give him. Where is the likeness? God suffered for men; the Lord, for the servant; the Just, for the sinners. Where is the equality? For the very reason that the servant has nothing else to give the Lord, God in his compassion accepts martyrdom as of equivalent value.
Homilies on the Psalms, Homily 40, Psalm 115 (116B) (FOTC 48)

449. If, in times of peace, I deny [Christ], what would I do in time of trial? I am not being tortured, nor set on fire, yet I deny Christ. If I were being stretched on the rack, were burning at the stake, what would I do?
Various Homilies, Homily 96—On the Persecution of Christians (FOTC 57)

PERSECUTION AND MARTYRDOM—*Conversion*

450. Let us be on guard, therefore, not to give way to anger against our persecutors, but let us grieve and lament for them, because it is another who is acting through them. ... He strikes me with blows; but I grieve and weep for my assailant, for I realize that he is being struck more piteously by the one working in him than I who receive the stinging blow from his hand. ... When we suffer anything at all from men, we may not yield to anger against them, but rather weep for them and perceive that it is the master of deceit forging his lies in them.
Homilies on the Psalms, Homily 43, Psalm 128 (129) (FOTC 48)

PERSECUTION AND MARTYRDOM—*Eternal Life*

451. The martyr who has been slain goes straight to heaven; the slayer, thus humiliated, falls himself in the very act of slaying.
Homilies on the Psalms, Homily 3, Psalm 7 (FOTC 48)

452. In martyrdom, I say, blood is shed, that the soul may be delivered from temptations; that it may forsake a short life and enter eternity; that it may leave all persecution behind and hasten to our Lord Jesus Christ for its crown.
Homilies on the Psalms: Second Series, Homily 73, Psalm 96 (97) (FOTC 57)

PERSECUTION AND MARTYRDOM—*Humility*

453. The unprotected are always the ready prey of tyranny, and the more humble the victim, the more does the persecutor offend against God.
Homilies on the Psalms, Homily 22, Psalm 93 (94) (FOTC 48)

454. I beg of you, let there be greater rivalry among us in the monastery in seeking to know how we may triumph over the devil, how we may fast, deplore our sins, prevent our thoughts from drawing us into the captivity of lust, be patient over every injury; how not to revile when a brother has wronged us, but how we may strive to conquer him with the humility that we have learned from Christ."
Homilies on the Psalms: Second Series, Homily 69, Psalm 91 (92) (FOTC 57)

PERSECUTION AND MARTYRDOM—*Justice*

455. Any man who lives in justice and has merited to be among the Lord's loving servants shall enter through this gate, for the Lord does not seek the blood of those who bear witness to him, but the faith through which they shed it.
Various Homilies, Homily 94—On Easter Sunday (FOTC 57)

PERSECUTION AND MARTYRDOM—*Love*

456. Consider what a truly amazing thing love is. If we suffer martyrdom in the hope that our mortal remains will be honored by men, and if in pursuit of accolades from the masses, we fearlessly spill our blood, and give our money and possessions away until we are penniless, we deserve not so much a reward as a penalty; these acts are the tortures merited by perfidy more than the crown of victory.
Commentary on Galatians, Book Three (Galatians 5.7–6.18), 5.13b-14 (FOTC 121)

Persecution and Martyrdom—*Sacrifice*

457. Martyrs, too, when they are being slaughtered, when they are being crucified, are yielding the harvest of their land.
Homilies on the Psalms: Second Series, Homily 64, Psalm 84 (85) (FOTC 57)

458. If we, therefore, want to be strangers to the teachings of this generation, and live our lives detached from the ways of the world, let us submit to persecutions and tribulations.
Various Homilies, Homily 91—On the Exodus (*The Vigil of Easter*) (FOTC 57)

459. Time and again, we have averred that Christians always suffer persecution. This world is in the power of the evil one. Our adversary, the devil, rules in the world, and do we think that we shall escape persecution? Besides, what is there that is not a source of persecution to the Christian? Everything that is of the world holds endless torment for him. Is it any wonder that others persecute us if we have determined to serve Christ? Even our parents do. Everyone who does not share our beliefs, harasses and hates us. Should we be surprised if we are the object of universal malevolence?
Various Homilies, Homily 96—On the Persecution of Christians (FOTC 57)

Persecution and Martyrdom—*Satan*

460. Does it not seem evident to you that during the persecution when the devil was persecuting Christians, when he was slaying martyrs, he was himself struck down in his very act of slaying?
Homilies on the Psalms, Homily 3, Psalm 7 (FOTC 48)

Poverty

POVERTY—*Condemnation*

461. It is not possible to have wealth both on earth and in hell.
Various Homilies, Homily 86—On the Gospel of Luke 16.19–31 (*The Rich Man and Lazarus*) (FOTC 57)

POVERTY—*Detachment*

462. Truly, this life is a dream, a dream of riches; for when we seem to have them within our grasp, immediately they slip away.
Homilies on the Psalms, Homily 9, Psalm 75 (76) (FOTC 48)

POVERTY—*Discipleship*

463. When the evils have been forsaken, one must do good things. For a wallet is more easily despised than the will. Many who abandon wealth do not follow the Lord. But he follows the Lord who is his imitator and walks in his footsteps.
Commentary on Matthew, Book Three (Matthew 16.13–22.40), 19.21 (FOTC 117)

POVERTY—*Eternal Life*

464. The Lord and Savior did not say that the rich will not enter the kingdom of heaven, but that they will enter with difficulty.
Homilies on the Psalms, Homily 16, Psalm 83 (84) (FOTC 48)

465. The saints in the present world are but pilgrims on earth, with no desire for material possessions; their property, all of it, is in heaven...
Homilies on the Psalms: Second Series, Homily 66, Psalm 88 (89) (FOTC 57)

POVERTY—*Freedom*

466. Let the greedy hear this, let him hear that the one who is enrolled by the name of Christian cannot serve Christ and riches at the same time. And, yet, he did not say: he who *has* riches, but: he who *serves* riches. For he who is a slave of riches guards his riches, like a slave; but the one who has shaken off the yoke of slavery distributes them, like a master.
Commentary on Matthew, Book One (Matthew 1.1–10.42), 6.24 (FOTC 117)

POVERTY—*Grace*

467. He who has given up material things for the Savior's sake will receive spiritual things.
Commentary on Matthew, Book Three (Matthew 16.13–22.40), 19.29–30 (FOTC 117)

POVERTY—*Happiness*

468. Unhappy the rich with whom the devil lurks!
Homilies on the Psalms, Homily 3, Psalm 7 (FOTC 48)

469. Happy the people who possess Christ in the place of all riches.
Homilies on the Psalms, Homily 54, Psalm 143 (144) (FOTC 48)

POVERTY—*Humility*

470. But lest anyone think that the Lord is preaching the kind of poverty that is sometimes borne by necessity, he has added "in spirit," that you might understand humility, not indigence. "Blessed are the poor of spirit" (Matthew 5.3), who on account of the Holy Spirit are poor voluntarily.
Commentary on Matthew, Book One (Matthew 1.1–10.42), 5.3 (FOTC 117)

POVERTY—*Idolatry*

471. You should see the teachers of heretics doing nothing but ogling their treasures. They gaze fondly at their possessions and scorn Christ the pauper.
Homilies on the Psalms, Homily 54, Psalm 143 (144) (FOTC 48)

POVERTY—*Injustice*

472. It is almost impossible for the rich man to be rich without robbing the poor.
Homilies on the Psalms, Homily 3, Psalm 7 (FOTC 48)

POVERTY—*Judgment*

473. The warriors against your people are heedless of the judgment that is to come.
Homilies on the Psalms, Homily 15, Psalm 82 (83) (FOTC 48)

POVERTY—*Love*

474. God does not consider the extent of property, but the disposition of the soul that renounces it; they who have given up little would have given up much just as promptly.
Homilies on the Gospel of Saint Mark on Various Topics, Homily 76 (II)—On Mark 1.13–31 (FOTC 57)

475. If we become martyrs, straightaway we are in Paradise; if we endure the pains of poverty, instantly, we are in Abraham's bosom. Blood has its own abode, and so does peace. Poverty, too, has its martyrdom; need well borne is martyrdom—but need suffered for the sake of Christ, and not from necessity. How many beggars there are who long to be rich men and, therefore, commit crime! Poverty of itself does not render one blessed, but poverty for the sake of Christ. Faith does not fear hunger. The lover of Christ has no fear of hunger; he who has Christ, with him possesses all riches.
Various Homilies, Homily 86—On the Gospel of Luke 16.19–31 (*The Rich Man and Lazarus*) (FOTC 57)

POVERTY—*Salvation*

476. [Jesus] became a poor man with men that no one might despair of salvation because of his poverty.
Homilies on the Psalms, Homily 35, Psalm 108 (109) (FOTC 48)

477. [Monks] do not have the wealth of the devil, but they have the poverty of Christ. … The devil promises a kingdom and wealth in order to destroy life; the Lord promises poverty in order to preserve it. We do nothing so very great if we renounce our possessions; Christ left his Father and the kingdom of heaven for our sake. … Christ, I say, was made a pauper for us.
Homilies on the Psalms, Homily 54, Psalm 143 (144) (FOTC 48)

POVERTY—*Service*

478. Surely, one does not serve God with devotion unless he despises the wealth of the world.
Homilies on the Psalms, Homily 38, Psalm 111 (112) (FOTC 48)

POVERTY—*Temptation*

479. The riches of others are torments to those who are in poverty.
Various Homilies, Homily 86—On the Gospel of Luke 16.19–31 (*The Rich Man and Lazarus*) (FOTC 57)

Prayer

480. Our prayer is works.
Homilies on the Psalms, Homily 1, Psalm 1 (FOTC 48)

481. God hears our voice in the morning; will he not hear us in the evening? Nor in the middle of the night?
Homilies on the Psalms, Homily 2, Psalm 5 (FOTC 48)

482. As long as I am wandering in the darkness of error, you do not hear me, but after the sun of justice has come into my heart, then you will.
Homilies on the Psalms, Homily 2, Psalm 5 (FOTC 48)

483. When we are in trouble, we are dejected and think of nothing but our trouble; yet the best recourse in time of affliction is to pray earnestly to God.
Homilies on the Psalms, Homily 10, Psalm 76 (77) (FOTC 48)

484. Whenever we lift up pure hands in prayer, without deliberate distractions and contention, we are playing to the Lord with a ten-stringed instrument.
Homilies on the Psalms, Homily 21, Psalm 91 (92) (FOTC 48)

485. When the ear of the body does not understand, the ear of the spirit does.
Homilies on the Psalms, Homily 22, Psalm 93 (94) (FOTC 48)

486. To bless the Lord, that is, to praise the Lord, brings, moreover, a blessing upon oneself.
Homilies on the Psalms, Homily 30, Psalm 103 (104) (FOTC 48)

487. [Prayer] is the Lord's weapon; that is our weapon, too, prayer. If ever anyone should persecute us and hate us, let us say likewise: in return for my love, they gave me calumny. But I, what did I do? I prayed.
Homilies on the Psalms, Homily 35, Psalm 108 (109) (FOTC 48)

488. The voice that cries to God does not come from the lips, but from the heart.
Homilies on the Psalms, Homily 59, Psalm 149 (FOTC 48)

Repentance

REPENTANCE—*Conscience*

489. Repentance is without limit. Wherever there is sin, always there is remorse of conscience… While time lasts, the door is always open to repentance, for however long you shall live, as long as you live, you will fall into sin.
Homilies on the Psalms: Second Series, Homily 72, Psalm 95 (96) (FOTC 57)

REPENTANCE—*Eternal Life*

490. Think of how much glory there awaits the penitent.
Homilies on the Psalms, Homily 34, Psalm 107 (108) (FOTC 48)

REPENTANCE—*Eternity*

491. Grant me a little time that I may repent for my sins, for in hell, no one has the power to confess his sins.
Homilies on the Psalms, Homily 30, Psalm 103 (104) (FOTC 48)

REPENTANCE—*Happiness*

492. Happy the man in whose heart Christ rises daily, and he will rise every day, if every day the sinner repents his sins, even slight ones.
Homilies on the Psalms, Homily 23, Psalm 95 (96) (FOTC 48)

REPENTANCE—*Hope*

493. O, you who sin grievously and despair of salvation, and think that because of the magnitude of your sins you cannot obtain pardon, I admonish you… to give thanks to the Lord, for he is good. Great are your sins, but great is the Lord who has pity on you. Confess your sins to the Lord; do penance, and do not despair of your salvation, for the Lord is compassionate. Give thanks to the Lord, you who have very great sins. Do not trust in your own strength, but trust in the mercy of the Lord. … It is not possible for anyone in hell to be sorry for his sins. While you are still in this world, I beg of you to repent. Confess and give thanks to the Lord, for in this world only is he merciful. … Here, he is compassionate kindness; there, he is Judge. Here, he reaches out his hand to the falling; there, he presides as Judge.
Homilies on the Psalms, Homily 32, Psalm 105 (106) (FOTC 48)

REPENTANCE—*Humility*

494. If our earth had not been thoroughly shaken and troubled, we would not be Christians. ... The Spirit of the Lord rests upon the lowly, the peaceful, and those who tremble at his words.
Homilies on the Psalms, Homily 10, Psalm 76 (77) (FOTC 48)

REPENTANCE—*Love*

495. Those who persevere in sin are those who are held in abhorrence by God, but those who abandon the ways of sin are loved by the Lord.
Homilies on the Psalms, Homily 2, Psalm 5 (FOTC 48)

REPENTANCE—*Mercy*

496. See how powerful repentance for sin is; it prevents the threatening wrath of God.
Homilies on the Psalms: Second Series, Homily 64, Psalm 84 (85) (FOTC 57)

REPENTANCE—*Patience*

497. We are admonished not to cut off a brother quickly. For it can happen that the one who today has been seduced by a harmful doctrine, tomorrow may come to his senses and begin to defend the truth.
Commentary on Matthew, Book Two (Matthew 11.2–16.12), 13.37 (FOTC 117)

REPENTANCE—*Peace*

498. There is no healing peace in a tearless security.
Homilies on the Psalms, Homily 18, Psalm 86 (87) (FOTC 48)

REPENTANCE—*Penance*

499. Unless you repent and do penance, the Lord will brandish his sword against you.
Homilies on the Psalms, Homily 3, Psalm 7 (FOTC 48)

500. Unhappy the man whom the Lord does not chastise. Anyone whom the Lord does not punish while he is sinning is most unfortunate.
Homilies on the Psalms, Homily 13, Psalm 80 (81) (FOTC 48)

501. God's love embraces both mercy and fidelity. If he were only merciful, he would be inviting us all to sin; if he loved only faithfulness, no one would have any hope of repentance. God, therefore, has recourse to both, and tempers one with the other. If you are a sinner, heed the mercy of God and do not despair, but do penance. If, on the other hand, you are just, do not grow careless because God is clement, for God is just and loves faithfulness.
Homilies on the Psalms, Homily 16, Psalm 83 (84) (FOTC 48)

REPENTANCE—*Prayer*

502. The very moment that I begin to withdraw from iniquity, that very moment do I merit your attention to my prayers.
Homilies on the Psalms, Homily 2, Psalm 5 (FOTC 48)

REPENTANCE—*Purity*

503. He calls you to repentance in order that you, who were a leper, may have Christ for your Guest.
Homilies on the Psalms, Homily 17, Psalm 84 (85) (FOTC 48)

504. First, repent and wash away sin with your tears; then, sing to the Lord.
Homilies on the Psalms, Homily 21, Psalm 91 (92) (FOTC 48)

505. One cannot praise the Lord if he is unfaithful, for it behooves the sinner to lament his sins, not sing to the Lord.
Homilies on the Psalms, Homily 48, Psalm 136 (137) (FOTC 48)

506. From repentance cleanliness is effected.
Homilies on the Psalms, Homily 57, Psalm 147 (147B) (FOTC 48)

507. When [the saints] were foolish, incredulous, erring, slaves to desires and pleasures of all sorts, stirring up trouble in greed and envy, they multiplied their weaknesses; when they were baptized and sanctified; when, converted to repentance, they abandoned their sins of the past; then, they made haste.
Homilies on the Psalms: Second Series, Homily 61, Psalm 15 (16) (FOTC 57)

REPENTANCE—*Salvation*

508. If [the wicked] repent and do penance, they too will be saved. When the Apostle Paul was persecuting Christ and his Church, he was wicked.
Homilies on the Psalms, Homily 1, Psalm 1 (FOTC 48)

509. No matter what sin you have committed, repent, and in every respect, you will be saved.
Homilies on the Psalms, Homily 23, Psalm 95 (96) (FOTC 48)

510. He who is covered with shame is close to salvation, for when one is sincerely disturbed and in confusion, he begins to repent.
Homilies on the Psalms, Homily 35, Psalm 108 (109) (FOTC 48)

REPENTANCE—*Sincerity*

511. Torments, not the disposition of your soul, force repentance.
Various Homilies, Homily 86—On the Gospel of Luke 16.19–31 (*The Rich Man and Lazarus*) (FOTC 57)

REPENTANCE—*Sovereignty*

512. Because we are the sons of man, and have lost the right to be the sons of God and have been perverted; on that account, guide us, that once again we may become your children.
Homilies on the Psalms, Homily 19, Psalm 89 (90) (FOTC 48)

513. We give God praise and glory when we acknowledge our sins before him.
Homilies on the Psalms, Homily 30, Psalm 103 (104) (FOTC 48)

The Resurrection

THE RESURRECTION—*Historicity*

514. He who does not know before the Passion, does know after the Resurrection.
Homilies on the Gospel of Saint Mark on Various Topics, Homily 84 (X)—On Mark 13.32–33 and 14.3–6 (FOTC 57)

515. What has taken place historically is very clear; the sepulcher was hewn out of rock (we must give a literal interpretation first), very hard rock; he was laid in a new tomb, and a great stone was rolled to the entrance; and a military guard was stationed there to prevent any possibility of stealing him away. Now all this precaution took place that the power of God would be all the more manifest when he arose from the dead. ... The extreme caution of the scribes and [Pontius Pilate] has rendered service to our faith. ... God cannot be shut in; God cannot be confined in a sepulcher. He who made heaven and earth, in the palm of whose hand rest heaven and earth, ... he who, as I was saying, balances the universe, cannot be contained in a single sepulcher.
Various Homilies, Homily 87—On the Gospel of John 1.1–14 (FOTC 57)

516. It is not that the Lord spent the whole of three days and three nights in the nether world. Rather, the three days and three nights refer to part of the day of preparation, part of the Lord's day, and the whole of the Sabbath day.
Commentary on Matthew, Book Two (Matthew 11.2–16.12), 12.39–40 (FOTC 117)

The Resurrection—*Joy*

517. A son of the Resurrection, moreover, can never be sorrowful.
Homilies on the Psalms, Homily 16, Psalm 83 (84) (FOTC 48)

518. {God's} kindness has always been manifest to {his} faithful servants, but never has it been so clear and lavish, as when the Redeemer of all rose from the dead for the salvation of each and every one. … After the joy of the Resurrection of our Lord, by which we believe that we have been redeemed and shall rise again on the day of judgment, we rejoice for the rest of our days and exult with the fullness of trust.
Homilies on the Psalms: Second Series, Homily 67, Psalm 89 (90) (FOTC 57)

The Resurrection—*Primacy*

519. Just as the Virgin Mary, the Mother of the Lord, holds the first place among all women, even so, [Easter Sunday] is the mother of days among all days.
Various Homilies, Homily 93—On Easter Sunday (FOTC 57)

520. The Lord's day, however, the day of the Resurrection, the day of Christians, is our day. It is called the Lord's day because on this day the Lord ascended to the Father as Victor; but when the heathens call it the day of the sun, we are most happy to acknowledge their

title, for today has risen: "the sun of justice with its healing wings" (Malachi 3.20).
Various Homilies, Homily 94—On Easter Sunday (FOTC 57)

The Resurrection—*Providence*

521. Unless the Lord who was prostrate in his Passion stands by us, unless he rises up who was sleeping in death, we cannot overcome our enemies.
Homilies on the Psalms: Second Series, Homily 71, Psalm 93 (94) (FOTC 57)

522. Authority has been given to him who a little earlier was crucified, who was buried in a tomb, who lay there dead, who afterward was resurrected.
Commentary on Matthew, Book Four (Matthew 22.41–28.20), 28.18 (FOTC 117)

The Sacraments

The Sacraments—*Anointing of the Sick*

523. Nothing is ever made sacred except by anointing.
Homilies on the Psalms, Homily 45, Psalm 132 (133) (FOTC 48)

The Sacraments—*Baptism*

524. Anyone, therefore, who is not sincere in the reception of baptism proves it at the waters of strife and discord.
Homilies on the Psalms, Homily 13, Psalm 80 (81) (FOTC 48)

525. As long as you do not come to blood and water, you cannot be saved.
Homilies on the Psalms, Homily 17, Psalm 84 (85) (FOTC 48)

526. Baptism remits sin, and, as it were, releases the soul from prison; it cannot, however, bestow the kingdom of heaven, for if one does not enter through faith and good works, he cannot be sure of salvation.
Homilies on the Psalms, Homily 47, Psalm 135 (136) (FOTC 48)

527. Truly, with the coming of the Lord Savior, all our guilt is wholly removed by baptism.
Homilies on the Psalms: Second Series, Homily 64, Psalm 84 (85) (FOTC 57)

528. Even as John the Baptist was the precursor of the Lord Savior, so was the baptism of John the Baptist the precursor of the baptism of the Savior. The former was given in repentance; the latter, in grace. On that occasion, repentance is granted; on that occasion, pardon; on this, victory is conferred.
Homilies on the Gospel of Saint Mark on Various Topics, Homily 75 (I)—On the Beginning of the Gospel of Saint Mark (1.1–12) (FOTC 57)

529. Until we receive baptism, our eyes are closed; we do not discern the divine.
Homilies on the Gospel of Saint Mark on Various Topics, Homily 75 (I)—On the Beginning of the Gospel of Saint Mark (1.1–12) (FOTC 57)

530. You are about to approach baptism. O, happy you, who are to be reborn in Christ, who are going to receive the garment of Christ, who are to be buried with him, that you may rise again with him!
Homilies on the Gospel of Saint Mark on Various Topics, Homily 83 (IX)—On Mark 11.15–17 (FOTC 57)

531. Those who are going to be baptized must believe in the Father, the Son, and the Holy Spirit.
Homilies on the Gospel of Saint Mark on Various Topics, Homily 84 (X)—On Mark 13.32–33 and 14.3–6 (FOTC 57)

532. [The Son of God] came for baptism, and he is holier than the one who baptizes.
Various Homilies, Homily 89—For Epiphany (*On the Gospel Text of the Lord's Baptism and on Psalm 28*) (FOTC 57)

533. The Savior accepted baptism from John for three reasons: first, in order that, since he had been born man, he might fulfill all the justice and humility of the Law; second, so that by his own baptism he might give approval to John's baptism; third, so that by sanctifying the waters of the Jordan by the descent of the dove, he might show forth the coming of the Holy Spirit in the [baptismal] bath of believers.
Commentary on Matthew, Book One (Matthew 1.1–10.42), 3.13 (FOTC 117)

534. First, they teach all nations, then they dip in water those who have been taught. For it is not possible that the body receives the sacrament of baptism unless the soul first receives the truth of the faith. Now they are baptized in the name of the Father, and of the Son, and of the Holy Spirit. Thus, there is one gift from those whose divinity is one. And the name of Trinity is one God.
Commentary on Matthew, Book Four (Matthew 22.41–28.20), 28.19 (FOTC 117)

535. Those who believe, who are baptized in the Trinity, must do everything that has been taught.
Commentary on Matthew, Book Four (Matthew 22.41–28.20), 28.20 (FOTC 117)

536. Although {Christ} was free from sin, he received the baptism of repentance in the Jordan River ostensibly to inculcate in others, who are worldly, the need to be cleansed through baptism and be born as sons by a new spiritual adoption.
Commentary on Galatians, Book Two (Galatians 3.10–5.6), 4.4–5 (FOTC 121)

THE SACRAMENTS—*Christ*

537. How much more are all the acts of the Savior sacraments for us.
Homilies on the Gospel of Saint Mark on Various Topics, Homily 81 (VII)—On Mark 11.1–10 (FOTC 57)

THE SACRAMENTS—*Confirmation*

538. Nothing is ever made sacred except by anointing.
Homilies on the Psalms, Homily 45, Psalm 132 (133) (FOTC 48)

THE SACRAMENTS—*The Holy Eucharist*

539. Do you want to receive food from the Lord? Do you want to feed upon the Lord himself, your Lord and Savior? … He is both Lord and Bread. He exhorts us to eat and he is himself our food.
Homilies on the Psalms, Homily 13, Psalm 80 (81) (FOTC 48)

540. What is mortal necessarily requires food that is mortal; what is immortal, the soul, requires immortal food.
Homilies on the Psalms, Homily 42, Psalm 127 (128) (FOTC 48)

541. We, indeed, accept such exegesis, for it is truly the Body of Christ and truly the Blood of Christ.
Homilies on the Psalms, Homily 55, Psalm 145 (146) (FOTC 48)

542. May we perpetuate in our heart the inscription and the memory of {the Lord's} Passion.
Homilies on the Psalms: Second Series, Homily 61, Psalm 15 (16) (FOTC 57)

543. The Savior is, then, our food and drink (truly, we eat his flesh and drink his blood).
Homilies on the Psalms: Second Series, Homily 61, Psalm 15 (16) (FOTC 57)

544. The fruit of our earth is the Bread of Life, who was born for us at Bethlehem. Bethlehem, in fact, means "house of bread," and this is the Bread that came forth in Bethlehem, that coming down from heaven, was made for us; Bread into whose mystery angels desire to look.
Homilies on the Psalms: Second Series, Homily 64, Psalm 84 (85) (FOTC 57)

545. Now the hour bids us approach the Body of the Savior, the true Lamb, with pure and chaste conscience in the unity of peace, that worthily we may partake of the heavenly Bread, through Christ Jesus our Lord.
Homilies on the Psalms: Second Series, Homily 65, Psalm 87 (88) (FOTC 57)

546. Just as Melchizedek had done, the priest of the Most High God, when he offered bread and wine in the prefiguration of him, he too would present it in the truth of his own body and blood.
Commentary on Matthew, Book Four (Matthew 22.41–28.20), 26.26–27 (FOTC 117)

547. For the saint, every day is the day of Christ's Resurrection, and he always feeds on the Lord's flesh. But days for fasting and gathering together for worship were instituted by prudent men for the sake of those who leave more time for the world than for God, and are

unable, or rather unwilling, to congregate in church every moment of their lives, or to put the offering of the sacrifice of their prayers to God ahead of their human activities. For how few people are there who always observe at least these few regulations about the times of prayer or fasting? Thus, ... we are allowed to fast always, to pray always, and to celebrate unceasingly and joyfully in the Lord's day by receiving his body.
Commentary on Galatians, Book Two (Galatians 3.10–5.6), 4.10–11 (FOTC 121)

THE SACRAMENTS—*Holy Orders*

548. Appreciate the dignity of the priesthood! Priests speak, and in priests, it is God praising his Son.
Homilies on the Psalms, Homily 35, Psalm 108 (109) (FOTC 48)

549. If Judas [Iscariot] lost his office of Apostle, let priest and bishop be on guard, lest they, too, lose their ministry. If an Apostle fell, more easily is it possible for a monk to fall.
Homilies on the Psalms, Homily 35, Psalm 108 (109) (FOTC 48)

550. It is part of the priestly office to be able to teach the people. ... It is the priest's duty to answer questions on the Law.
Homilies on the Gospel of Saint Mark on Various Topics, Homily 81 (VII)—On Mark 11.1–10 (FOTC 57)

551. What is the work of God if not to read Scripture, to preach in church, to aspire to the priesthood, and to serve before the altar of the Lord? But even these arise from a longing for praise if one is not very careful about guarding his heart.
Commentary on Galatians, Book Three (Galatians 5.7–6.18), 5.26 (FOTC 121)

The Sacraments—*Marriage*

552. The reward of marriage is the making of one flesh out of two. Chastity, when united with the Spirit, makes one spirit.
Commentary on Matthew, Book Three (Matthew 16.13–22.40), 19.5 (FOTC 117)

553. In the same way {the Apostle} Paul uses the words "impurity" and "debauchery" to cover every other conceivable lustful desire, including sexual relations within marriage, if these are not performed with a sense of modesty and respectability (as if God were watching), and then only for the purpose of procreation.
Commentary on Galatians, Book Three (Galatians 5.7–6.18), 5.19–21 (FOTC 121)

The Sacraments—*Penance*

554. Just as the body has wounds of various kinds, so also the soul has its passions and its wounds, and we must do penance in proportion to the nature of our sin. If a man makes confession of all his sins, he is acknowledging his sins to the Lord wholeheartedly. If, for example, someone has committed fornication, and he confesses only that, and is avaricious, or irascible, or a slanderer, or blasphemer, and is full of faults and vices, his confession is not sincere. The man who repents for all the sins and passions of his soul is the man who is able to say: I confess and give thanks to you, O Lord, with all my heart.
Homilies on the Psalms, Homily 49, Psalm 137 (138) (FOTC 48)

555. If… anyone sins, and does not repent, then he is long dead; he is not merely like those dead, but is actually dead.
Homilies on the Psalms, Homily 53, Psalm 142 (143) (FOTC 48)

556. Do you want to be clean? Do penance.
Homilies on the Psalms, Homily 57, Psalm 147 (147B) (FOTC 48)

557. Repent of your sins, and at that instant, you are converted to God.
Homilies on the Psalms, Homily 58, Psalm 148 (FOTC 48)

558. Happy the man whose sins are forgiven in baptism; second to baptism, however, penance is like a plank after a shipwreck. The penitent, too, may, therefore, be called happy. Granted, he is rescued with peril, but since he is rescued by his regret for sin, he is to be called happy.
Homilies on the Psalms: Second Series, Homily 64, Psalm 84 (85) (FOTC 57)

559. With humble submission, {we take} refuge in penance.
Homilies on the Psalms: Second Series, Homily 67, Psalm 89 (90) (FOTC 57)

560. It is good for man, first, to repent and confess his sins to the Lord, and when he has acknowledged his sins, then, sing praise to him, for by penance he has merited the power to burst forth into the praise of God, unrestrained by the consciousness of sin.
Homilies on the Psalms: Second Series, Homily 69, Psalm 91 (92) (FOTC 57)

561. When I confess my sins, when I do not trust in my own power, when I do not boast that I am strong, at once, {God's} kindness is a hand to sustain me.
Homilies on the Psalms: Second Series, Homily 71, Psalm 93 (94) (FOTC 57)

562. Our penitence is perfume to the Savior. Just see how great is the compassionate kindness of the Savior! Our sins are malodorous, putrid; still, if we do penance for our wrongdoings, if we weep over them, our foul offenses become the strongest fragrant perfume of the Lord.
Homilies on the Gospel of Saint Mark on Various Topics, Homily 76 (II)—On Mark 1.13–31 (FOTC 57)

563. Those whose sins are forgiven are called men.
Commentary on Matthew, Book One (Matthew 1.1–10.42), 6.14 (FOTC 117)

564. There is a fault of silence on the part of the one who was unwilling to preach to those who would do penance.
Commentary on Matthew, Book Two (Matthew 11.2–16.12), 11.23 (FOTC 117)

THE SACRAMENTS—*Sacramentals*

565. Do we have the proper reverence for sacramentals?
Homilies on the Psalms, Homily 45, Psalm 132 (133) (FOTC 48)

566. No one marked with the sign of the cross on his forehead can be struck by the devil; he is not able to efface this sign, only sin can.
Homilies on the Gospel of Saint Mark on Various Topics, Homily 84 (X)—On Mark 13.32–33 and 14.3–6 (FOTC 57)

THE SACRAMENTS—*Sacred Scripture*

567. Our Lord changed the beginning of evangelical baptism and the sacraments of the Law into the sacraments of the Gospel.
Homilies on the Gospel of Saint Mark on Various Topics, Homily 75 (I)—On the Beginning of the Gospel of Saint Mark (1.1–12) (FOTC 57)

568. The concluding chapters of Ezekiel are devoted to a description of the building of a temple, situated on a high mountain. This description serves as a foreshadowing of the sacraments of the future Church to be established after many centuries have run their course.
The Dialogue Against the Pelagians, Book One, paragraph 39 (FOTC 53)

THE SACRAMENTS—*Sacrifice*

569. Just as a soldier never ceases to train for battle and prepares in sham warfare for the real wounds that are to come, every Christian must exercise self-restraint at all times, but especially when the enemy is near at hand with his well-trained hosts marshalled against us. It is always necessary for God's servants to fast, but it is even more imperative when we are preparing for the sacrifice of the Lamb, for the sacrament of Baptism, for the Body and Blood of Christ.
Various Homilies, Homily 90—On Lent (*First Sunday in Lent*) (FOTC 57)

Saintliness and Virtue

SAINTLINESS AND VIRTUE—*The Cardinal Virtues (Fortitude, Justice, Prudence, and Temperance)*

570. [Wisdom] is of great advantage to us; fortitude is valuable in resisting persecution; finally, temperance and chastity are indispensable in preventing us from losing our souls.
Homilies on the Psalms, Homily 5, Psalm 14 (15) (FOTC 48)

571. [The virtues] gratify the one who possesses them; justice does not give pleasure to the one possessing it, but instead pleases others. If I am wise, wisdom delights me; if I am brave, my fortitude comforts me; if I have been chaste, my chastity is my joy.
Homilies on the Psalms, Homily 5, Psalm 14 (15) (FOTC 48)

572. Moderation differs from self-control in that moderation is present in those who are spiritually mature and bountifully virtuous. The one who has self-control, however, is indeed on his way to becoming virtuous but has not yet arrived at his goal because sinful desires still

invade his thoughts and pollute the very core of his mind, though they do not overcome him or entice him to translate thought into action.
Commentary on Galatians, Book Three (Galatians 5.7–6.18), 5.22–23 (FOTC 121)

SAINTLINESS AND VIRTUE—*Chastity and Self-Control*

573. Those who guard their innocence, who have no vices, delight in the Lord.
Homilies on the Psalms, Homily 7, Psalm 67 (68) (FOTC 48)

574. When we have been liberated from the passion of lust, that is, from its effects, then we begin to acquire the virtues.
Homilies on the Psalms, Homily 7, Psalm 67 (68) (FOTC 48)

575. When our passions subside, and the sun of our iniquity sets, the Sun of justice rises for us; the Lord reigns over us, and in us takes up his abode.
Homilies on the Psalms, Homily 7, Psalm 67 (68) (FOTC 48)

576. When we do not commit murder, it is because our hands are held in check.
Homilies on the Psalms, Homily 8, Psalm 74 (75) (FOTC 48)

577. Let us beg God to make us kings, that we may rule over our flesh, that it be subject to us.
Homilies on the Psalms, Homily 9, Psalm 75 (76) (FOTC 48)

578. Anger, lust, and vengeful insult become an opportunity for me to gain victory, provided that I show self-restraint, stay silent for God's sake, and remember that God is watching over me as I endure each and every agitation of the passions and incitement to vice.
Commentary on Galatians, Book Three (Galatians 5.7–6.18), 6.10 (FOTC 121)

SAINTLINESS AND VIRTUE—*Contemplation*

579. I am not brooding over my anger, nor over my enemy; all my musing is of God. The night that is wont to be a time for rest, or for lust, is for me a time of pondering deeply upon virtue.
Homilies on the Psalms, Homily 10, Psalm 76 (77) (FOTC 48)

SAINTLINESS AND VIRTUE—*Conversion*

580. May our soul be in command, our body in subjection; then, Christ will come at once to make his abode with us. ... Every day Christ stands at the door of our hearts; he longs to enter. Let us open wide our hearts to him; then, he will come in and be our host and guest; he will dwell in us and sup with us.
Homilies on the Psalms, Homily 9, Psalm 75 (76) (FOTC 48)

581. If you are not holy, the way of God is not in you. ... The way, therefore, is the Son of God. The way of God, moreover, is only in the saintly man. If we want Christ to dwell in us, let us be saints, for the way of God is holiness.
Homilies on the Psalms, Homily 10, Psalm 76 (77) (FOTC 48)

582. Let them cease to exist as far as their evil is concerned, but let the good in them be saved.
Homilies on the Psalms, Homily 15, Psalm 82 (83) (FOTC 48)

583. The holy man sets his heart on ascending; the sinner, on descending.
Homilies on the Psalms, Homily 16, Psalm 83 (84) (FOTC 48)

584. The harp has many strings; if one is broken, it cannot play. So, too, the holy man; albeit he is a saint, if he be lacking in one virtue, he cannot give voice to his song.
Homilies on the Psalms, Homily 56, Psalm 146 (147A) (FOTC 48)

585. Let us beseech the Lord to walk with us, that he may be our companion in the perils of this life; and that by walking in our hearts pure of sin, he may delight always to dwell in us.
Homilies on the Psalms: Second Series, Homily 64, Psalm 84 (85) (FOTC 57)

586. The works of the Savior cannot be compared with the works of Beelzebub. The latter desires to hold the souls of men captive; the Lord wants them to be liberated. The one preaches idols; the other, the knowledge of the one of God. The one drags people to the vices; the other calls them back to the virtues.
Commentary on Matthew, Book Two (Matthew 11.2–16.12), 12.30 (FOTC 117)

587. Happy is he who walks in the way of virtue, provided of course that he reaches perfection in it. There is no point in abstaining from vice unless you embrace moral excellence, because when it comes to noble pursuits, the beginning is not as praiseworthy as the end. A grape goes through many stages between the vine and the winepress.
Commentary on Galatians, Book Two (Galatians 3.10–5.6), 4.15–16 (FOTC 121)

588. Those who wish to live in Christ Jesus must seek virtue and flee from vice.
Commentary on Galatians, Book Two (Galatians 3.10–5.6), 5.6 (FOTC 121)

589. In Scripture, a load can be taken in either a bad sense, to refer to people who are weighed down with heavy sins, or in a good sense, to speak of those who bear the light load of the virtues.
Commentary on Galatians, Book Three (Galatians 5.7–6.18), 5.10b (FOTC 121)

SAINTLINESS AND VIRTUE—*Discipleship*

590. The saintly man teaches holiness to others who are not holy.
Homilies on the Psalms, Homily 38, Psalm 111 (112) (FOTC 48)

SAINTLINESS AND VIRTUE—*Eternal Life*

591. Paradise is the homeland of the saints.
Homilies on the Psalms: Second Series, Homily 66, Psalm 88 (89) (FOTC 57)

592. Knowledge and works of the present life are types of the future blessedness.
Commentary on Matthew, Book Four (Matthew 22.41–28.20), 25.17 (FOTC 117)

SAINTLINESS AND VIRTUE—*Faith*

593. The Lord is the guardian of truth for all eternity. Someone has lied against us, and the liar is given more credence than we who are telling the truth. We must not despair; the Lord keeps faith forever.
Homilies on the Psalms, Homily 55, Psalm 145 (146) (FOTC 48)

594. We know that we cannot be saved by the works of the Law, but by faith in Christ. We have believed in Christ so that our faith in him might give us what the Law could not. We abandoned the Law in which we could not have been saved, and we have gone over to faith, in which the devotion of a pure heart is demanded. … If I was able to be saved by keeping the old Law instead of by having faith in him, then I have believed in Christ in vain.
Commentary on Galatians, Book One (Galatians 1.1–3.9), 2.15 (FOTC 121)

SAINTLINESS AND VIRTUE—*Fortitude*

595. The hour bids me be silent, but the greatness of the mysteries compels me to speak.
Homilies on the Psalms, Homily 56, Psalm 146 (147A) (FOTC 48)

596. If it is our desire, therefore, to be of the Lord's inheritance and portion, let us be brave and strong; ... Let there be nothing weak in us, nothing inconstant, nothing unworthy of an heir, for Christ glories in his saints.
Homilies on the Psalms: Second Series, Homily 61, Psalm 15 (16) (FOTC 57)

SAINTLINESS AND VIRTUE—*Good Works*

597. Notice that our good works cry out to the Lord even when we are silent.
Homilies on the Psalms, Homily 10, Psalm 76 (77) (FOTC 48)

598. Through each virtue, Christ is born. ... Whoever performs virtuous acts, engenders virtue.
Homilies on the Psalms, Homily 18, Psalm 86 (87) (FOTC 48)

599. The work of the saints is the praise of God. Christ is not praised in word, but in works; he does not heed the voice, but the deed.
Homilies on the Psalms, Homily 25, Psalm 97 (98) (FOTC 48)

600. Unless we are mountains of virtue, we cannot ascend into heaven.
Homilies on the Psalms, Homily 45, Psalm 132 (133) (FOTC 48)

601. God, the omnipotent, does not need man's goods, nor do our virtuous acts contribute to the perfection of God, since increment is impossible to him, but whatever we produce by toil and bring forth

in labor, that he exacts and takes from us in order to give back to us what he has received.
Homilies on the Psalms: Second Series, Homily 61, Psalm 15 (16) (FOTC 57)

602. Magnanimity does not consist in words, but in deeds.
Various Homilies, Homily 95—On Obedience (FOTC 57)

603. Perfect blessedness is to fulfill in deed what you teach in word.
Commentary on Matthew, Book One (Matthew 1.1–10.42), 5.19 (FOTC 117)

604. Jesus proves that they are refuted who claim the knowledge of the Lord without works.
Commentary on Matthew, Book One (Matthew 1.1–10.42), 7.21 (FOTC 117)

SAINTLINESS AND VIRTUE—*Hope*

605. Neither should the virtuous man be secure nor the sinner despair of his salvation, for in each of them there should be both fear and hope.
Homilies on the Psalms, Homily 32, Psalm 105 (106) (FOTC 48)

SAINTLINESS AND VIRTUE—*Humility*

606. Even if he is an emperor, even if he is a governor, if he is a bishop, if he is a priest (for these are dignitaries in the Church), whoever he is, if he is evil, he is nothing in the sight of the saint.
Homilies on the Psalms, Homily 5, Psalm 14 (15) (FOTC 48)

607. As the Lord is inebriated in his Passion, his saints are inebriated every day in the ardor of their faith, inebriated in the Holy Spirit.

You, who yesterday were heaping together gold, today, you are throwing it away. Are you not a madman to those who do not know what it is all about?
Homilies on the Psalms, Homily 13, Psalm 80 (81) (FOTC 48)

608. When we are worldly, we do not exalt God; but, if from earthly beings, we become heavenly beings, then we give glory to God.
Homilies on the Psalms, Homily 34, Psalm 107 (108) (FOTC 48)

SAINTLINESS AND VIRTUE—*Joy*

609. May we not look upon him as sorrowful, but as rejoicing. May we not behold him sorrowful because of our sins, but rejoicing in our virtues.
Homilies on the Psalms, Homily 6, Psalm 66 (67) (FOTC 48)

SAINTLINESS AND VIRTUE—*Love*

610. It is not virtue, but the motive of virtue, that has a reward with God.
Commentary on Matthew, Book One (Matthew 1.1–10.42), 6.2 (FOTC 117)

SAINTLINESS AND VIRTUE—*Perseverance*

611. God has entered us as contestants in a race course where it is our lot to be always striving.
Homilies on the Psalms, Homily 16, Psalm 83 (84) (FOTC 48)

612. All the Commandments of the Lord demand effort. Without labor and toil, we cannot possess the kingdom of heaven.
Homilies on the Psalms, Homily 22, Psalm 93 (94) (FOTC 48)

613. The present life is a contest, not a canticle. An army never sings unless it is on its way to victory; consequently, I am not free to sing in the present combat. When I win the victory, then, I shall sing.
Homilies on the Psalms, Homily 54, Psalm 143 (144) (FOTC 48)

614. God made this world an arena that here we may strive against the devil, against sin, in order to receive our crown in heaven. Why did he ordain a contest? Could not he save us without the struggle? He gave us, as it were, a Master of contests; he gave us a stadium in which to carry on our wrestling against vices, so that afterwards he may crown us meritoriously, not as those who sleep, but as those who labor. ... That is why he gave a place for the contest: that he who had given us the rules of the contest might afterwards give us a blessing.
Homilies on the Psalms: Second Series, Homily 63, Psalm 83 (84) (FOTC 57)

615. [God] does not give a crown to the slothful, but to those who toil.
Homilies on the Psalms: Second Series, Homily 68, Psalm 90 (91) (FOTC 57)

616. No matter what the virtues, they are not acquired without difficulty. By great toil and effort, we reach the top of a mountain; how much more labor is necessary to reach heaven?
Homilies on the Psalms: Second Series, Homily 71, Psalm 93 (94) (FOTC 57)

617. Let us flee from earthly things and hasten toward heavenly things.
Commentary on Matthew, Book Two (Matthew 11.2–16.12), 13.31–32 (FOTC 117)

618. We have the whole duration of our lives for perpetual celebration in Christ, and not some fleeting and minuscule portion of it.
Commentary on Galatians, Book Two (Galatians 3.10–5.6), 4.10–11 (FOTC 121)

Saintliness and Virtue—*Providence*

619. Now, one who cries "help" is himself making an effort to be saved, for it is not while we are sleeping that God helps us, but while we are exerting ourselves.
Homilies on the Psalms, Homily 12, Psalm 78 (79) (FOTC 48)

Saintliness and Virtue—*Repentance*

620. If the sun sets, do we think that we are going to be everlasting? It is certainly amazing how so much light and such brightness, that the whole world is illuminated, in the flash of a moment is gone. Let us pray, however, that the sun of justice may not set for us. ... Allegorically, when the sun of justice sets for us, we are in total darkness; then the beasts come after us, and the lion roars in its wild passion to snatch up and devour us. ... The man who has fallen into sin should not be downcast, but let him repent. The sun of justice will rise again, and all the beasts will be put to flight and his sins with them, and he will be restored to his state before his fall. Once more for him, the sun of justice shall rise. ... Very important it is, then, that we pursue the works of justice every minute of our lives.
Homilies on the Psalms, Homily 30, Psalm 103 (104) (FOTC 48)

Saintliness and Virtue—*Service*

621. The virtues of the saints are gifts to God.
Homilies on the Psalms, Homily 7, Psalm 67 (68) (FOTC 48)

Saintliness and Virtue—*Sovereignty*

622. Because you reign in me and sin does not, that is why you are my God. You are my God because my stomach is not my God, gold is

not my God, lust is not my God. Since you are virtue and I desire to possess virtue, you are my God, you are my virtue.
Homilies on the Psalms, Homily 2, Psalm 5 (FOTC 48)

623. Praise the Lord, all you servants of the Lord, who are not the servants of sin, but the servants of our Lord; all you servants of the Lord who have one Lord only, God; all you servants of the Lord who are not governed by anger, who are not swayed by passion, who are not ruled by other sins. They who are not under the dominance of vice are under the dominion of the Lord.
Homilies on the Psalms, Homily 46, Psalm 133 (134) (FOTC 48)

624. God, alone, truly is Lord, who requires service of his servants only that he may have occasion to bestow more gifts upon them. Along with this, we learn the lesson that if the Savior pleads in our behalf…, surely, we ought all the more to pray for ourselves, because however fast we may run, without him, we cannot arrive at the goal.
Homilies on the Psalms: Second Series, Homily 61, Psalm 15 (16) (FOTC 57)

625. This is consummate justice in man, not to impute any virtue that he can attain to himself, but rather to the Lord, the Giver.
The Dialogue Against the Pelagians, Book One, paragraph 13 (FOTC 53)

Satan and Temptation

SATAN AND TEMPTATION—*Arrogance*

626. All the devil wants is to hold his head up high, but he cannot.
Homilies on the Psalms, Homily 3, Psalm 7 (FOTC 48)

627. Notice that the man who holds his head high in arrogance hates God.
Homilies on the Psalms, Homily 15, Psalm 82 (83) (FOTC 48)

628. Let the arrogance of those be struck down who regard themselves as saints and have no fear of the presence of the Judge.
Commentary on Matthew, Book Four (Matthew 22.41–28.20), 24.28 (FOTC 117)

629. He who is cautious and wary can avoid sins for awhile, but he who is secure in his own justice opposes God, and, deprived of his help, he is subject to the snares of the enemy.
The Dialogue Against the Pelagians, Book Two, paragraph 24 (FOTC 53)

SATAN AND TEMPTATION—*Concupiscence*

630. In the soul there is always the spark of concupiscence. Just as, if there is a spark of fire in ashes but nothing to feed it, the spark is there nonetheless but does not burst into flame; so, too, the spark of fire in our thought is checked if it is not fanned into flame by the excesses of the flesh. We all have this spark.
Homilies on the Psalms, Homily 33, Psalm 106 (107) (FOTC 48)

631. It is hard to find the man who is not gripped by concupiscence, not shaken by temptations.
Homilies on the Gospel of Saint Mark on Various Topics, Homily 80 (VI)—On Mark 9.1–7 (FOTC 57)

SATAN AND TEMPTATION—*Fallenness*

632. The devil always has his bow ready, and he is ever alert to shoot his arrows and strike us down.
Homilies on the Psalms, Homily 3, Psalm 7 (FOTC 48)

633. They who have been inebriated from the cup of the devil fall headlong in their drunkenness.
Homilies on the Psalms, Homily 15, Psalm 82 (83) (FOTC 48)

634. The devil is the hunter, eager to lure our souls into perdition. The devil is master of many snares, deceptions of all kinds. Avarice is one of his pitfalls, detraction is his noose, fornication is his bait. ... As long as we are in a state of grace, our soul is at peace; but once we begin to play with sin, then our soul is in trouble and is like a boat tossed about by the waves.
Homilies on the Psalms, Homily 20, Psalm 90 (91) (FOTC 48)

635. In whatever kind of sin I walk, I am walking the devil's way, and Christ is not reigning in me. My mind is vain and preoccupied with distractions of all sorts. I am in one place, and my mind is wandering all over the world.
Homilies on the Psalms, Homily 55, Psalm 145 (146) (FOTC 48)

636. The enemy wars against us, and never retreats, even in defeat, but always lies in ambush, ready to shoot his arrows at the upright of heart from his secret hiding place.
The Dialogue Against the Pelagians, Book Three, paragraph 1 (FOTC 53)

SATAN AND TEMPTATION—*Freedom in Christ*

637. Anyone tempted by wanton desire cannot escape sin unless the Lord appear and release him.
Homilies on the Psalms, Homily 31, Psalm 104 (105) (FOTC 48)

638. [The devil] holds us tight within his grip, not because he loves, but because he hates. ... Great the majesty, great the power of the blood of the Lord, which liberated us from the clasp of the devil. ... The blood of Christ has broken the unyielding clutch of the devil. He did not want to let go of us, but the Lord poured forth

his blood as the oil of mercy, and through his blood set us free.
Homilies on the Psalms, Homily 33, Psalm 106 (107) (FOTC 48)

639. The presence of the Savior is torment for demons.
Commentary on Matthew, Book One (Matthew 1.1–10.42), 8.29 (FOTC 117)

640. Christ cannot do evil works, and the devil cannot do good works.
Commentary on Matthew, Book Two (Matthew 11.2–16.12), 12.35 (FOTC 117)

SATAN AND TEMPTATION—*His Defeat*

641. The devil has as many heads as there are sins. … God smashes the devil's head so completely that all his strength to goad sinners is gone.
Homilies on the Psalms, Homily 7, Psalm 67 (68) (FOTC 48)

642. The Lord, yes, was crucified, but the devil died. The Lord fulfilled the divine mystery, and the Victor was visible; the devil was not visible, but was slain spiritually...
Homilies on the Psalms, Homily 32, Psalm 105 (106) (FOTC 48)

643. If Christ is the way of the just, the way of the wicked is the devil, but the way of the wicked, he will destroy. The way, then, of all the wicked is the devil; him, he will destroy, but he will preserve us who were walking in the midst of that way, but now do so no longer.
Homilies on the Psalms, Homily 55, Psalm 145 (146) (FOTC 48)

SATAN AND TEMPTATION—*Lust*

644. They whose hearts are burning with lust and passion are the very ones whom the devil conquers.
Homilies on the Psalms, Homily 3, Psalm 7 (FOTC 48)

SATAN AND TEMPTATION—*Pride*

645. Just as anyone who tosses a stone straight up into the air, and is foolish enough not to move out of its way, is struck on the head and wounded by his own stone; in the same way, the devil downs himself by his own arrogance; the pride that exalts him is the same pride that defeats him.
Homilies on the Psalms, Homily 3, Psalm 7 (FOTC 48)

SATAN AND TEMPTATION—*Resistance to Evil*

646. God did not delay in the desert, but passed through it.
Homilies on the Psalms, Homily 7, Psalm 67 (68) (FOTC 48)

647. It is impossible for anyone, even though he be a saint, to pass through this world without temptation.
Homilies on the Psalms, Homily 7, Psalm 67 (68) (FOTC 48)

648. We, however, must not follow our own inclinations.
Homilies on the Psalms, Homily 15, Psalm 82 (83) (FOTC 48)

649. The man who is wary of snares through fear can readily escape them.
Homilies on the Psalms, Homily 18, Psalm 86 (87) (FOTC 48)

650. While the athlete sleeps, he loses the victory.
Homilies on the Psalms, Homily 34, Psalm 107 (108) (FOTC 48)

651. Not ordinarily does the devil make his attack through grave faults, but through slight ones, that in some way or another he may gain admittance, win his victory, and ultimately impel his man to greater vices. Not through fornication or avarice, but through lesser sins, he secures an entrance. ... O unhappy race of men! We seek excuse for our sin by saying, "Nature got the better of me," and all

the while, it has been in our power to sin or not to sin. We are always justifying ourselves and saying: 'I did not want to sin, but lust overwhelmed me; that woman came to me; she herself made the advances; she touched me; she said this or that to me; she called me'; and, while we ought to be doing penance and crying, "Lord, I have sinned," we excuse ourselves instead, and yoke sin to sin. We all have the same kind of body, but with our own particular difficulties. ... Would you know that we have the same bodies as the saints? ... We all have our own struggles, therefore, and it is in proportion to his struggles that each one receives his reward.
Homilies on the Psalms, Homily 51, Psalm 140 (141) (FOTC 48)

652. It is not possible to keep the persecutions of the devil from resounding about the just man. If the Lord himself was scourged and harassed by tribulations and temptations, who of the just will not be stung with the devil's lash? ... The devil has certainly produced an uproar on the outside, and has tried to arouse sensuous passions, but the tent of the soul, or the mind which is the tabernacle of faith, he does not subvert.
Homilies on the Psalms: Second Series, Homily 68, Psalm 90 (91) (FOTC 57)

653. We may not give assent to the testimony of demons.
Homilies on the Gospel of Saint Mark on Various Topics, Homily 76 (II)—On Mark 1.13–31 (FOTC 57)

654. As soon as the devil is aware that his sheep are determined to withdraw from his flock, he rages in madness, and in fury gathers all his forces against them, reckoning that whatever is saved for Christ is lost to him; ... Because he knows that we want to become children of God, he plots to take us by surprise, and, like a slimy serpent, coils himself about our feet to keep us from mounting to heaven. If with vile cunning he has dared to tempt the Lord, how much more boldly will he presume to deceive us?
Various Homilies, Homily 90—On Lent (*First Sunday in Lent*) (FOTC 57)

655. *Then he was led into the desert by the Spirit.* It is scarcely to be doubted that {the Lord} was led by the Holy Spirit. ... He is not led unwillingly, or as a captive, but with the intention of doing battle.
Commentary on Matthew, Book One (Matthew 1.1–10.42), 4.1 (FOTC 117)

656. The devil ... is always desiring the downfall of everyone. ... He can persuade, but he cannot cast down.
Commentary on Matthew, Book One (Matthew 1.1–10.42), 4.6 (FOTC 117)

657. Temptation precedes so that victory may follow.
Commentary on Matthew, Book One (Matthew 1.1–10.42), 4.11 (FOTC 117)

658. The devil can be a helper and an inciter of evil thoughts, but he cannot be their author. Yet, he always lies in wait and kindles small sparks in our thoughts with his own tinder.
Commentary on Matthew, Book Two (Matthew 11.2–16.12), 15.19 (FOTC 117)

659. Every believer knows what is harmful to himself, and by what his heart can be stirred up and often tempted. It is better to lead a solitary life than on account of the necessities of the present life to lose eternal life.
Commentary on Matthew, Book Three (Matthew 16.13–22.40), 18.8–9 (FOTC 117)

660. Whoever knows and asks a question, not with the wish to learn, but out of a zeal to find out whether the one who is to respond knows, he approaches not as a learner, but as a tempter.
Commentary on Matthew, Book Three (Matthew 16.13–22.40), 22.34–37 (FOTC 117)

661. It is impossible for a human soul not to be tempted. This is why in the Lord's prayer we say "Lead us not into temptation" (Matthew 6.13, Luke 11.4) that we are unable to bear. We are not refusing to face temptation altogether, but praying for the strength of endurance in temptation. Therefore, in the present passage, he does not say: "Watch and pray" that you not be tempted, but "that you not enter into temptation," that is, that temptation not overcome and conquer you and hold you in its nets.
Commentary on Matthew, Book Four (Matthew 22.41–28.20), 26.41 (FOTC 117)

662. For the Savior was tempted in every way, just as we are, yet he was without sin. This was so that, after being shown by his own example how difficult it is to attain victory in the flesh, he would be in a position to commiserate and empathize with our weaknesses (cf. Hebrews 4.15).... If the Savior was tempted, who can be sure of crossing the seas of this life unscathed by temptation?
Commentary on Galatians, Book Three (Galatians 5.7–6.18), 6.1 (FOTC 121)

SATAN AND TEMPTATION—*Slavery to Sin*

663. Every sinner is held captive.
Homilies on the Psalms, Homily 17, Psalm 84 (85) (FOTC 48)

664. Vice and sin are the gates of death.
Homilies on the Psalms, Homily 18, Psalm 86 (87) (FOTC 48)

665. To err is human, but to lay snares is diabolical.
The Apology Against the Books of Rufinus, Book Three, paragraph 33 (FOTC 53)

Scripture

SCRIPTURE—*The Canon*

666. One river comes forth from the throne of God—the grace of the Holy Spirit—and this grace of the Holy Spirit is found in the river of the Sacred Scriptures. This river, moreover, has two banks, the Old Testament and the New Testament, and the tree planted on both sides is Christ.
Homilies on the Psalms, Homily 1, Psalm 1 (FOTC 48)

667. You will find the grace of the Holy Spirit in the two Testaments.
Homilies on the Psalms, Homily 7, Psalm 67 (68) (FOTC 48)

668. We interpret mountains in two ways: in the Old Testament as prophets; in the New, as apostles. ... We were all sitting in darkness and in the shadow of death, and the Lord shone upon us from his eternal mountains, that is, from the prophets and the Apostles.
Homilies on the Psalms, Homily 9, Psalm 75 (76) (FOTC 48)

669. The two wheels are the New and the Old Testament; the Old moves within the New, and the New within the Old.
Homilies on the Psalms, Homily 10, Psalm 76 (77) (FOTC 48)

670. In the Old Testament, the divine mysteries point to the Gospels, and in the New Testament back to the law.
Homilies on the Psalms, Homily 19, Psalm 89 (90) (FOTC 48)

671. The four Gospels are summed up in the decalogue. Everything contained in the decalogue is fulfilled in the four Gospels; hence, the Old Law does not contradict the authority of the Gospels.
Homilies on the Psalms, Homily 22, Psalm 93 (94) (FOTC 48)

672. The two Testaments fortify each other, and in so doing, break the heretics' net.
Homilies on the Psalms: Second Series, Homily 60, Psalm 10 (11) (FOTC 57)

673. What {the prophets} utter is the Lord's, and not their own; that which the Lord proclaims by their mouths, he speaks as through an instrument.
Homilies on the Psalms: Second Series, Homily 66, Psalm 88 (89) (FOTC 57)

674. The Old Law lifted men up a little from the ground, but it could not carry them to heaven.
Homilies on the Gospel of Saint Mark on Various Topics, Homily 75 (I)—On the Beginning of the Gospel of Saint Mark (1.1–12) (FOTC 57)

675. Because the Law was only the beginning of the Covenant; the Gospel is the fulfillment.
Homilies on the Gospel of Saint Mark on Various Topics, Homily 75 (I)—On the Beginning of the Gospel of Saint Mark (1.1–12) (FOTC 57)

676. The faith of the Law has confirmed the faith of the Gospel.
Homilies on the Gospel of Saint Mark on Various Topics, Homily 76 (II)—On Mark 1.13–31 (FOTC 57)

677. Separating the Law and the prophets and the Gospel [is] a thing which cannot be done. ... There is, indeed, but one tent for the Gospel, the Law, and the prophets. Unless they dwell together, they cannot be in harmony.
Homilies on the Gospel of Saint Mark on Various Topics, Homily 80 (VI)—On Mark 9.1–7 (FOTC 57)

678. When I read the Gospel and see there testimony from the Law and the prophets, I contemplate Christ alone. I have looked at Moses and Elias only that I might understand them as they speak of Christ.

Finally, when I come to the splendor of Christ, and behold, as it were, the exceedingly brilliant light of the bright sun, I cannot see the light of the lamp. Can a lamp give light if you light it in the daytime? If the sun is shining, the light of the lamp is not visible, so when Christ is present, the Law and the prophets, by comparison, are not even visible. ... Rather I am praising them, for they proclaim Christ; I so read the Law and the prophets that I do not remain in them, but through them arrive at Christ.

Homilies on the Gospel of Saint Mark on Various Topics, Homily 80 (VI)—On Mark 9.1–7 (FOTC 57)

679. It is plainly shown that only the four Gospels ought to be received.
Commentary on Matthew, Preface (FOTC 117)

680. Both in the Old and in the New Testament, the following should always be observed: When a more majestic vision appears, at first, fear is expelled. Thus, when the mind has been made calm in this way, the things that are said can be heard.
Commentary on Matthew, Book Four (Matthew 22.41–28.20), 28.10 (FOTC 117)

681. The universal Church... maintains that one divine plan unites the Old and New Testaments, and does not distinguish in time those whom it binds together by condition. We have all been built upon the foundation of the prophets and Apostles, and are stabilized by the cornerstone, our Lord Jesus Christ.
Commentary on Galatians, Book Two (Galatians 3.10–5.6), 4.1–2 (FOTC 121)

682. Anyone who is a Christian reads Moses and the prophets. He knows that their writings led the people's way in shadows and images, and that they were written for the sake of us, on whom the fulfillment of the ages has come.
Commentary on Galatians, Book Two (Galatians 3.10–5.6), 4.17–18 (FOTC 121)

683. It is no wonder that the Old Covenant, which is on Mount Sinai in Arabia, and near the present city of Jerusalem, was intended to be temporary, seeing that [Hagar's] wandering is different from perpetual possession; that the name Mount Sinai means "tribulation," while Arabia means "death"; and that, by contrast, the Jerusalem which is above and is free and the mother of saints shows that the Jerusalem of the present is earthly and submerged in lowliness and baseness.
Commentary on Galatians, Book Two (Galatians 3.10–5.6), 4.24b-26 (FOTC 121)

684. I recall that I once corrected the edition of the Septuagint translators from the Greek, and made it accessible to our brethren. ... It is a different matter, to be sure, if they close their eyes to what is said, and seek to revile me, and refuse to imitate the zeal and good will of the Greeks, who read carefully the Septuagint translators, when the Gospel of Christ is already flourishing... When I had translated it a second time, according to the Hebrew itself, I made the following remark: "In the case of all of the books of Sacred Scripture, I am forced to answer the slanders of my adversaries, who charge that my translation is a rebuke to the Septuagint translators..."
The Apology Against the Books of Rufinus, Book Two, paragraphs 27 and 29 (FOTC 53)

685. We do not say this because we wish to rebuke the Septuagint translators, but because the authority of the Apostles and of Christ is greater; and wherever the Septuagint translators are not at variance with the Hebrew, there the Apostles took their examples from the translation; but where they differ, they quoted in Greek what they had learned from the Hebrews. ... From all of this, it is clear that the edition of the Septuagint translators, which has been established by the antiquity of its readers, is useful to the churches, since the Gentiles heard of the coming of Christ before he came; and that the other translators are not to be reproved because they translated not their own, but sacred volumes...
The Apology Against the Books of Rufinus, Book Two, paragraphs 34 and 35 (FOTC 53)

SCRIPTURE—*The Church*

686. What is this way of yours? The reading of Holy Scripture. Direct my steps, therefore, lest I stumble in the reading of your Word through which I desire to enter your Church, for everyone whose understanding of Holy Writ is faulty falls down in the path of God.
Homilies on the Psalms, Homily 2, Psalm 5 (FOTC 48)

SCRIPTURE—*Divine Inspiration*

687. All of Holy Writ is animated and held together by one [Holy] Spirit. It is not unlike a necklace held together by the union of its links, so that whichever link you pick up, another suspends from it.
Homilies on the Gospel of Saint Mark on Various Topics, Homily 76 (II)—On Mark 1.13–31 (FOTC 57)

SCRIPTURE—*Divine Revelation*

688. The Old Testament speaks of the Son in a hidden manner. In the Gospel, let us read openly of the manifestations of the Son.
Homilies on the Psalms, Homily 3, Psalm 7 (FOTC 48)

689. Moreover, because you do not know the Scriptures, you do not know Christ, who is the power of God and the wisdom of God.
Homilies on the Psalms, Homily 11, Psalm 77 (78) (FOTC 48)

690. Mark how our Lord instructs the soul by his own Word, and by recalling Scripture.
Various Homilies, Homily 86—On the Gospel of Luke 16.19–31 (*The Rich Man and Lazarus*) (FOTC 57)

691. The good pearls are the Law and the prophets and the knowledge of the Old Testament, but the one pearl of very great price is the

knowledge of the Savior and the concealed mystery of his Passion and Resurrection.
Commentary on Matthew, Book Two (Matthew 11.2–16.12), 13.45–46 (FOTC 117)

692. The Gospel is already in full splendor.
On the Perpetual Virginity of the Blessed Mary Against Helvidius, paragraph 22 (FOTC 53)

SCRIPTURE—*Interpretation and the Senses of Scripture*

693. Listen very attentively, for we want to interpret Holy Writ, not merely exercise our oratory.
Homilies on the Psalms, Homily 3, Psalm 7 (FOTC 48)

694. Where there is in the soul the knowledge of Scripture and its doctrine, that soul is the dwelling place of God.
Homilies on the Psalms, Homily 9, Psalm 75 (76) (FOTC 48)

695. It is not my desire to reclaim rhetoric, but to penetrate the meaning of Holy Writ.
Homilies on the Psalms, Homily 11, Psalm 77 (78) (FOTC 48)

696. We certainly are not engaged in airing a point of rhetoric, but are endeavoring to understand and explain what the Holy Spirit said.
Homilies on the Psalms, Homily 15, Psalm 82 (83) (FOTC 48)

697. So much for what Scripture says; learn now what it means.
Homilies on the Psalms, Homily 15, Psalm 82 (83) (FOTC 48)

698. We are ascending upward gradually to a mystical understanding.
Homilies on the Psalms, Homily 18, Psalm 86 (87) (FOTC 48)

699. Just see how full of mystical meaning Sacred Scripture is!
Homilies on the Psalms, Homily 18, Psalm 86 (87) (FOTC 48)

700. Everything we say, we ought to confirm from Sacred Scripture.
Homilies on the Psalms, Homily 26, Psalm 98 (99) (FOTC 48)

701. Great… is the responsibility of him who expounds on the Word of the Lord.
Homilies on the Psalms, Homily 38, Psalm 111 (112) (FOTC 48)

702. Prove your claim from Sacred Scripture, for we must not make an assertion unless it has been adduced from, and confirmed by, Scripture.
Homilies on the Psalms, Homily 43, Psalm 128 (129) (FOTC 48)

703. Let us read Sacred Scripture, and day and night, let us ponder over its every syllable, every letter; let us analyze and discuss it.
Homilies on the Psalms, Homily 44, Psalm 131 (132) (FOTC 48)

704. Give me any churchman trained in divine Scripture. Let Eunomius come, let Arius come and try to adduce anything from the prophets against us, does not our churchman stand firm as a bar? Does he not refute them with the fixed firmness of a bar? … Whenever you see a man of the Church in debate, do not imagine that it is he who is debating; no, he who gives strength to him is carrying on the disputation.
Homilies on the Psalms, Homily 57, Psalm 147 (147B) (FOTC 48)

705. The man who possesses the sword of Holy Writ, what else does he need?
Homilies on the Psalms, Homily 59, Psalm 149 (FOTC 48)

706. Scripture speaks in terms of our human frailty, that we may the more easily understand.
Homilies on the Psalms: Second Series, Homily 65, Psalm 87 (88) (FOTC 57)

707. We have to know the very flesh and blood of Holy Writ, so that, when we understand exactly what is written, we can grasp its import. … Consequently, we must not be careless in reading Scripture.
Homilies on the Gospel of Saint Mark on Various Topics, Homily 78 (IV)—On Mark 8.1–9 (FOTC 57)

708. The historical facts are clear, the literal sense is obvious; we must search into its spiritual message.
Homilies on the Gospel of Saint Mark on Various Topics, Homily 79 (V)—On Mark 8.22–26 (FOTC 57)

709. If we consider the literal interpretation only, it does not make any sense.
Homilies on the Gospel of Saint Mark on Various Topics, Homily 79 (V)—On Mark 8.22–26 (FOTC 57)

710. We shall inquire into the significance of the words in order to fathom the mystery contained in the text.
Homilies on the Gospel of Saint Mark on Various Topics, Homily 80 (VI)—On Mark 9.1–7 (FOTC 57)

711. We are not denying the historical event, but prefer a spiritual explanation. Nor are we merely expressing our own opinion; we follow the judgment of the Apostles.
Homilies on the Gospel of Saint Mark on Various Topics, Homily 80 (VI)—On Mark 9.1–7 (FOTC 57)

712. If we ponder it spiritually, Holy Writ, that is, the clothing of the Word, is transformed immediately, and becomes as white as snow.
Homilies on the Gospel of Saint Mark on Various Topics, Homily 80 (VI)—On Mark 9.1–7 (FOTC 57)

713. Do you see how the spiritual interpretation benefits our soul?
Homilies on the Gospel of Saint Mark on Various Topics, Homily 80 (VI)—On Mark 9.1–7 (FOTC 57)

714. If I read Genesis, Exodus, Leviticus, Numbers, and Deuteronomy, as long as I read carnally, I seem to be down below, but if I grasp their spiritual significance, I am climbing to the top of the mountain. … When I read Holy Writ and appreciate something more sublimely in its spiritual sense, neither do I want to descend, to come down to the lowly; I want only to build in my heart a tabernacle for Christ, the Law, and the prophets. But Jesus, who came to save that which had been lost, not to save saints, but those who are in sin, knows that if the human race is to be on the mountain, mankind will not be saved unless he descends to the earthly.
Homilies on the Gospel of Saint Mark on Various Topics, Homily 80 (VI)—On Mark 9.1–7 (FOTC 57)

715. Nor, on the other hand, should we interpret [Holy Writ] as do the heretics, who with their allegories and nebulous explanations turn it into perverted dogma, tear out its very sinews, extract the life-blood of its truth, and smother it with figurative obscurities. Rather, let us understand Holy Writ, historically, yes, just as it is written; however, let us fire it with the flame of the Holy Spirit and unfold with spiritual discernment whatever in it seems incongruous or obscure when taken literally.
Various Homilies, Homily 91—On the Exodus (*The Vigil of Easter*) (FOTC 57)

716. Whatever is not perceived on the surface… is brought to light by exegetes only after they have well considered [Sacred Scripture] in painstaking investigation.
Various Homilies, Homily 91—On the Exodus (*The Vigil of Easter*) (FOTC 57)

717. Grasp the mystical meaning of Holy Writ.
Various Homilies, Homily 91—On the Exodus (*The Vigil of Easter*) (FOTC 57)

718. Let us call upon the Lord, probe the depths of his sacred writings, and be guided in our interpretation by other testimonies from Holy Writ. Whatever we cannot fathom in the deep recesses of the Old Testament, we shall penetrate and explain from the depth of the New Testament in the roar of God's cataracts—his prophets and Apostles.
Various Homilies, Homily 92—On Psalm 41 (42) (FOTC 57)

719. The devil therefore interprets the Scriptures badly.
Commentary on Matthew, Book One (Matthew 1.1–10.42), 4.6 (FOTC 117)

720. {Jesus} breaks the false arrows of the devil drawn from the Scriptures upon the true shields of the Scriptures.
Commentary on Matthew, Book One (Matthew 1.1–10.42), 4.7 (FOTC 117)

721. Do not accommodate the Scriptures to your meaning, but link your meaning to the Scriptures, and understand what follows.
Commentary on Matthew, Book One (Matthew 1.1–10.42), 10.29–31 (FOTC 117)

722. {Jesus} intermingles clear things with obscure things, so that by means of the things that they do understand, they might be challenged to the knowledge of those things which they do not understand. ... We need to be very cautious whenever the Lord explains his words. When he is questioned by his disciples, and then explains the inner meaning, we must not wish to understand anything more or less than what he has explained.
Commentary on Matthew, Book Two (Matthew 11.2–16.12), 13.3 (FOTC 117)

723. We are challenged to understand the things said, as often as we are admonished by {Jesus'} words.
Commentary on Matthew, Book Two (Matthew 11.2–16.12), 13.9 (FOTC 117)

724. The Apostles, as the scribes and secretaries of the Savior, impressed his words and commands on the fleshly tablets of their heart. They had been instructed in the mysteries of the heavenly kingdoms. They were powerful in the wealth of the householder, and from the treasury of their doctrines, they cast out new things and old. Thus, whatever they proclaimed in the Gospel, they proved by means of the words of the Law and the prophets.
Commentary on Matthew, Book Two (Matthew 11.2–16.12), 13.52 (FOTC 117)

725. We should not suppose that the essence of the Gospel is in the words rather than in the actual meaning of Scripture, or on the surface rather than in the innermost parts, or in the leaves of mere words rather than in the root of reason. ... Scripture is advantageous to its hearers when it is spoken with Christ, when it is proclaimed with the Father, and when the preacher introduces it with the Spirit. The devil also speaks about Scripture, and all the heresies, according to Ezekiel, take material from it and sew together pillows which they place under the elbow of every age.
Commentary on Galatians, Book One (Galatians 1.1–3.9), 1.11–12 (FOTC 121)

726. Whenever the Apostles quote from the Old Testament, it is my custom to revert to the sources of these quotations, and to scrutinize the quotations in their original context.
Commentary on Galatians, Book Two (Galatians 3.10–5.6), 3.10 (FOTC 121)

727. Allegory is properly part of the art of grammar. As children in school, we learn how to differentiate it from metaphor and other figures of speech. It sets out one thing in words, and signifies another in another sense. The books of the orators and poets are full [of examples of this device]. A good portion of the message of divine Scripture is also expressed through allegory.
Commentary on Galatians, Book Two (Galatians 3.10–5.6), 4.24a (FOTC 121)

728. Even if the Law is to be taken allegorically (as we believe, and as Paul teaches it should be), it was established in deference not to what the reader wants, but to the authority of the one writing it down.
Commentary on Galatians, Book Two (Galatians 3.10–5.6), 4.24b-26 (FOTC 121)

729. There are many styles of compositions, and... not only do the ideas vary, but even the phraseology of Scripture, depending upon the nature of the subject matter.
The Apology Against the Books of Rufinus, Book One, paragraph 15 (FOTC 53)

730. It is one thing to be a prophet, quite another matter to be a translator. In the one case, the spirit foretells what is to come; in the other, learning and abundance of words translate what is known. ... What we write after {Christ's} Passion and Resurrection is not so much prophecy as it is history. For things that are heard are narrated in one style; things that are seen, in another style. What we understand better, we also express better.
The Apology Against the Books of Rufinus, Book Two, paragraph 25 (FOTC 53)

Scripture—*The Psalms*

731. The Psalter is like a stately mansion that has only one key to the main entrance. Within the mansion, however, each separate chamber has its own key. Even though the great key to the grand entrance is the Holy Spirit, still each room without exception has its own smaller key. Should anyone accidentally confuse the keys and throw them out and then want to open one of the rooms, he could not do so until he found the right one. Similarly, the Psalms are each like single cells, every one with its own proper key.
Homilies on the Psalms, Homily 1, Psalm 1 (FOTC 48)

732. Pluck the chords of the psaltery in noble acts.
Homilies on the Psalms, Homily 7, Psalm 67 (68) (FOTC 48)

733. Just as the psaltery is composed of many strings, and if one should be broken, the instrument as such is useless; so, too, in our actions, if we transgress one Commandment, our psaltery is broken. *Homilies on the Psalms*, Homily 34, Psalm 107 (108) (FOTC 48)

SCRIPTURE—*Reflection*

734. If [man] reads with true spiritual insight, he gathers the fruit. *Homilies on the Psalms*, Homily 1, Psalm 1 (FOTC 48)

735. The word "cry" in Scripture does not refer to the cry of the voice, but the cry of the heart. *Homilies on the Psalms*, Homily 2, Psalm 5 (FOTC 48)

736. He who runs in haste to higher things carries within himself your Word. *Homilies on the Psalms*, Homily 10, Psalm 76 (77) (FOTC 48)

737. We have a most precious treasure in vessels of clay symbolizing the homely words of the Scriptures. *Homilies on the Psalms*, Homily 11, Psalm 77 (78) (FOTC 48)

738. So you see that the knowledge of Holy Writ, training in its lessons and performing its works, lightens for us our days of adversity. *Homilies on the Psalms*, Homily 22, Psalm 93 (94) (FOTC 48)

739. He who understands the Sacred Scriptures, who meditates constantly on the law of the Lord, and contemplates the things of heaven, he is the one who sings to God. He, moreover, who possesses all virtue and is skilled in good works, fashions, as it were, a harp of virtues and sings praise to the Lord. *Homilies on the Psalms*, Homily 31, Psalm 104 (105) (FOTC 48)

740. There are some who insist on saying, "I have no need for Sacred Scripture; the fear of God is enough for me." That is, therefore,

precisely why we affirm that, just as there are foods for the body, so there are, likewise, foods for the soul, namely, the Sacred Scripture.
Homilies on the Psalms, Homily 42, Psalm 127 (128) (FOTC 48)

741. We read the Scriptures; we commit the Psalms to memory; we master the Gospels; we expound the prophets; but we must not do this so as to win praise and glory in the presence of our brothers, but to please Christ, that his Word may resound from our lips.
Homilies on the Psalms, Homily 46, Psalm 133 (134) (FOTC 48)

742. The sinner, granted that he has sinned, granted that he has fallen, nevertheless, if he is near water, that is, if he reads the Sacred Scriptures and listens to the Divine Word from a holy man, his soul revives, and he is converted unto repentance.
Homilies on the Psalms, Homily 48, Psalm 136 (137) (FOTC 48)

743. Even heretics... when they turn to the Scriptures, are swallowed up immediately by the Rock, that is, by Christ, and are converted to him.
Homilies on the Psalms, Homily 51, Psalm 140 (141) (FOTC 48)

744. The divine Word is exceedingly rich, containing within itself every delight.
Homilies on the Psalms, Homily 57, Psalm 147 (147B) (FOTC 48)

745. I wish that we, too, might eat more of the corn bread of Holy Writ, so that there would be less left over for us to learn.
Homilies on the Gospel of Saint Mark on Various Topics, Homily 78 (IV)—On Mark 8.1–9 (FOTC 57)

746. If anyone follows the letter, and is completely of the earth, and looks at the ground in the manner of brute beasts, he is unable to see Jesus in a shining vestment, but for him who follows the Word of God and ascends the mountain, climbs to the top, for him, Jesus is instantly transfigured, and his garments shine exceedingly.

Homilies on the Gospel of Saint Mark on Various Topics, Homily 80 (VI)—On Mark 9.1–7 (FOTC 57)

747. If one does not feed on the Word of God, he does not live.
Commentary on Matthew, Book One (Matthew 1.1–10.42), 4.4 (FOTC 117)

748. In the Law, there is retribution; in the Gospel, grace; in the Law, faults are corrected; in the Gospel, the beginnings of sins are removed.
Commentary on Matthew, Book One (Matthew 1.1–10.42), 5.38–39 (FOTC 117)

749. Whenever the Passion is read in the Scriptures, we are gathered together, and through it, we can come to the Word of God.
Commentary on Matthew, Book Four (Matthew 22.41–28.20), 24.28 (FOTC 117)

750. Divine Scripture is edifying even when read, but it is much more profitable if it goes from written characters on a page to an audible voice, with the one teaching through an epistle giving instruction to listeners as if he were there in person. The living voice has great power. It resonates from the mouth of its author and is delivered with that characteristic intonation with which it was generated in his heart.
Commentary on Galatians, Book Two (Galatians 3.10–5.6), 4.20 (FOTC 121)

751. Take note of how many people quarrel among themselves about Scripture and make an athletic contest out of God's Word. They provoke one another and become envious if they are defeated; these people are desirous of empty glory.
Commentary on Galatians, Book Three (Galatians 5.7–6.18), 5.26 (FOTC 121)

Seeking Good

SEEKING GOOD—*Courage*

752. It is a less serious sin to pursue evil which you assumed was good than to lack the courage to defend what you know for certain is good.
The Dialogue Against the Pelagians, Preface, paragraph 2 (FOTC 53)

SEEKING GOOD—*Honor*

753. I say to you…, honor your parents insofar as they do not hinder your service to the Lord, your General.
Various Homilies, Homily 85—On the Gospel of Matthew 18.7–9 (FOTC 57)

SEEKING GOOD—*Kindness*

754. Kindness, or agreeableness…, is a virtue which is gentle, charming, peaceful, adept at getting along with all good people; it attracts others to close acquaintanceship with itself; it is soft-spoken and well-mannered. Furthermore, the Stoics define it as a virtue whose goal is to do good voluntarily.
Goodness is not much different from kindness, because its goal is also to do good voluntarily. But it does differ in that it can be more somber… it is not pleasant company, and it does not attract everyone to it by its pleasantness.
Commentary on Galatians, Book Three (Galatians 5.7–6.18), 5.22–23 (FOTC 121)

SEEKING GOOD—*Love*

755. Freedom to sin is not the fruit of faith in Christ. Rather, a willingness to do good works is enhanced by love for one's faith. We do good deeds not because we fear the Judge, but because we know that they are pleasing to him in whom we believe.
Commentary on Galatians, Book One (Galatians 1.1–3.9), 3.2 (FOTC 121)

SEEKING GOOD—*Providence*

756. We progress little by little toward perfection, and receive the adoption which we formerly lost.
Commentary on Galatians, Book Two (Galatians 3.10–5.6), 4.3 (FOTC 121)

SEEKING GOOD—*Truth*

757. Christ, who is Truth, holds up his shield, that the shield of Truth may vanquish falsehood and deceit.
Homilies on the Psalms, Homily 20, Psalm 90 (91) (FOTC 48)

758. The teachings of the philosophers [Socrates, Plato, and Aristotle] only intensified hunger for truth, rather than satisfied it.
Homilies on the Psalms, Homily 33, Psalm 106 (107) (FOTC 48)

759. [The woman with the hemorrhage's] touch on the hem of [Jesus'] garment was the cry of a believing heart. ... The Lord gives us gracious hearing when not simply our voice, but our distress, calls out to him.
Homilies on the Psalms, Homily 33, Psalm 106 (107) (FOTC 48)

SEEKING GOOD—*Virtue*

760. It will not be sufficient for us to shun evil unless we seek good.
Homilies on the Psalms, Homily 1, Psalm 1 (FOTC 48)

761. It is not enough for us to restrain from doing evil, unless we shall also do good.
Homilies on the Psalms, Homily 5, Psalm 14 (15) (FOTC 48)

762. Whatever is of profit to the soul is never too much; the good is never enough, if indeed, it is good.
Homilies on the Psalms, Homily 19, Psalm 89 (90) (FOTC 48)

763. What benefit is there in calling upon {the Lord} with your voice when you deny him by your deeds?
Commentary on Matthew, Book Four (Matthew 22.41–28.20), 25.11 (FOTC 117)

764. Everything we say, do, or think is sown in two fields, the flesh and the Spirit. If the things proceeding from our hand, mouth, and heart are good, they will overflow with the fruits of eternal life because they were sown in the Spirit. If the field of the flesh welcomes evil, it will sprout up a field of destruction for us.
Commentary on Galatians, Book Three (Galatians 5.7–6.18), 6.8 (FOTC 121)

Sin

SIN—*Bitterness*

765. God is sweet by nature; they who move him to bitterness are sinners, and they make God bitter for themselves. God does not

change his nature, but sinners themselves make God their bitterness.
Homilies on the Psalms, Homily 7, Psalm 67 (68) (FOTC 48)

Sin—*Captivity*

766. Wherever there is sin, there is captivity; wherever captivity, there is destruction and need for restoration.
Homilies on the Psalms: Second Series, Homily 72, Psalm 95 (96) (FOTC 57)

767. Once the soul has been possessed by envy, it is very difficult for it to receive virtue; it is almost impossible to restore the soul that envy has mastered.
Homilies on the Gospel of Saint Mark on Various Topics, Homily 76 (II)—On Mark 1.13–31 (FOTC 57)

768. The poison of envy can indeed be overcome, but it is put to rest with difficulty.
Commentary on Matthew, Book Four (Matthew 22.41–28.20), 22.46 (FOTC 117)

769. The kingdom of God cannot reign in the soul where sin reigns.
Commentary on Galatians, Book Three (Galatians 5.7–6.18), 5.19–21 (FOTC 121)

Sin—*Conversion*

770. We know that we suffer day by day, what is in our thoughts, and we blush with shame to reveal them. ... There is no one among men who has not sinned in thought.
Homilies on the Psalms, Homily 9, Psalm 75 (76) (FOTC 48)

771. My suffering is not from the cruelty of God, but from my own sins.
Homilies on the Psalms, Homily 10, Psalm 76 (77) (FOTC 48)

772. They who lay their foundation in malice, let them have no foundation at all, but let them roll back and forth and never remain fixed in their malice.
Homilies on the Psalms, Homily 15, Psalm 82 (83) (FOTC 48)

SIN—*Culpability*

773. Sin is not imputed except to him who knows he is committing it.
Homilies on the Psalms: Second Series, Homily 64, Psalm 84 (85) (FOTC 57)

774. Many offer just pretexts, as it were, as an excuse for their sins. They want to appear to be sinning by necessity, when in fact they are willfully delinquent. The Lord, who is the searcher of the heart and soul, looks intently at the future thoughts in each.
Commentary on Matthew, Book One (Matthew 1.1–10.42), 10.42 (FOTC 117)

775. Iniquity sits upon a leaden weight.
Commentary on Matthew, Book Two (Matthew 11.2–16.12), 11.28 (FOTC 117)

776. A man is a thief, and converts the Temple of God into a den of thieves, who seeks after financial gain from religion. His worship is not so much the worship of God as a pretext for business.
Commentary on Matthew, Book Three (Matthew 16.13–22.40), 21.12–13 (FOTC 117)

777. The man in whom there is detected artful malice cannot plead simplicity as an excuse.
The Apology Against the Books of Rufinus, Book One, paragraph 1 (FOTC 53)

Sin—*Denial of God*

778. There is a difference between the wicked and sinners. The wicked deny God altogether; the sinner acknowledges God and in spite of his acknowledgement commits sin.
Homilies on the Psalms, Homily 1, Psalm 1 (FOTC 48)

779. Holy Writ says the wicked man will be so unhappy that he is not even dust from the earth. Dust does not seem to have any substance, but it does, of course, have a kind of existence of its own. There is no body to it, yet what substance it does have is really by way of punishment. It is scattered here and there and is never in any one place; wherever the wind sweeps it, there its whole force is spent. The same is true of the wicked man. Once he has denied God, he is led by delusion wherever the breath of the devil sends him.
Homilies on the Psalms, Homily 1, Psalm 1 (FOTC 48)

Sin—*Example*

780. When we commit sin, moreover, we multiply sin by teaching others to do what we have done.
Homilies on the Psalms, Homily 1, Psalm 1 (FOTC 48)

Sin—*Fallenness*

781. As the saint is a temple of God, so the sinner makes of himself a tomb.
Homilies on the Psalms, Homily 7, Psalm 67 (68) (FOTC 48)

782. The wicked... by loving iniquity... detest their own soul.
Homilies on the Psalms: Second Series, Homily 60, Psalm 10 (11) (FOTC 57)

783. The sinner, however, sets his heart not on ascent, but on descent.
Homilies on the Psalms: Second Series, Homily 63, Psalm 83 (84) (FOTC 57)

SIN—*False Deities*

784. The man whose god is his stomach has a strange god. We have as many alien gods as we have vices and sins. I gave way to anger; anger is my god. I look upon a woman covetously; lust is my god. The thing that each one covets and worships, that is his god. The miser has a god of gold. ... Our God is virtue; the god of others is vice and sin.
Homilies on the Psalms, Homily 13, Psalm 80 (81) (FOTC 48)

SIN—*Lack of Faith*

785. Actually, when we commit sin, it is because our mind is wavering in faith. When we are giving way to anger, when we are detracting from the reputation of another, when we are committing murder, when we are yielding to fornication, just where is our faith?
Homilies on the Psalms, Homily 1, Psalm 1 (FOTC 48)

SIN—*Mortal and Venial Sins*

786. All sins must be avoided, to be sure, because all sins are contrary to God, but they vary in degree.
Homilies on the Psalms: Second Series, Homily 71, Psalm 93 (94) (FOTC 57)

Suffering

Suffering—*The Cross*

787. On the cross {Jesus} confounded the devil and his entire army. To be sure, Christ was crucified in his body, but on the cross, it was he who was crucifying there the devils. It was not a cross; it was a symbol of triumph.
Homilies on the Psalms, Homily 21, Psalm 91 (92) (FOTC 48)

788. In very truth, Christ came and made firm the human race that had been disturbed, so that it may not be moved for all eternity. His cross is the pillar of mankind; on this pillar he has built his house.
Homilies on the Psalms, Homily 23, Psalm 95 (96) (FOTC 48)

789. Let the faithful exult in the cross.
Homilies on the Psalms, Homily 59, Psalm 149 (FOTC 48)

790. The Gospel message sails briskly among its hearers until it comes to the subject of the cross, whereupon it hits a snag and is unable freely to move ahead any further.... The cross was called foolishness because God's folly is wiser than men, and it was called weakness and a stumbling block because the weakness of God is stronger than men.
Commentary on Galatians, Book Three (Galatians 5.7–6.18), 5.11 (FOTC 121)

791. We should realize that every boast pertaining to the cross to its glory and that whatever worthy deed is performed in [the name of] virtue is done for the sake of what the Lord suffered.
Commentary on Galatians, Book Three (Galatians 5.7–6.18), 6.14 (FOTC 121)

SUFFERING—*Eternal Life*

792. The magnitude of our tribulations determines the magnitude of our reward; as many wounds we endure, that many crowns do we merit.
Homilies on the Psalms, Homily 22, Psalm 93 (94) (FOTC 48)

SUFFERING—*Fasting*

793. Find comfort, O monk, in your fasting, since even the Lord fasted. I maintain that when the monk fasts, he becomes stronger from the fast; when his knees tremble from fasting, then is he strongest.
Homilies on the Psalms, Homily 35, Psalm 108 (109) (FOTC 48)

794. When we fast, when our faces are pale from fasting, when we are loathsome to look upon, let us realize that it is then that we appear more beautiful to Christ. ... In fasting there is victory, and in victory, triumph.
Homilies on the Psalms, Homily 35, Psalm 108 (109) (FOTC 48)

795. The weakness of the body is the vigor of the soul.
Homilies on the Psalms, Homily 41, Psalm 119 (120) (FOTC 48)

796. Fasting is, as it were, the foundation and [the support], of those who are mounting to greater heights.
Homilies on the Psalms, Homily 41, Psalm 119 (120) (FOTC 48)

797. We, too, if it is our desire to reach the Lord quickly, must multiply our infirmities, so that made weak in the flesh, we may become strong in the spirit.
Homilies on the Psalms: Second Series, Homily 61, Psalm 15 (16) (FOTC 57)

798. Your weapons are fasts; your battle is humility.
Homilies on the Gospel of Saint Mark on Various Topics, Homily 83 (IX)—On Mark 11.15–17 (FOTC 57)

799. Boasting about fasting is reprehensible.
Commentary on Matthew, Book One (Matthew 1.1–10.42), 9.14 (FOTC 117)

800. The custom of the Church comes to the Passion of the Lord and the Resurrection by means of the humbling of the flesh.
Commentary on Matthew, Book One (Matthew 1.1–10.42), 9.15 (FOTC 117)

SUFFERING—*Humility*

801. Christ is a pauper, let us blush with shame; Christ is lowly, let us be ashamed; Christ was crucified; he did not rule: he was crucified in order to rule. He conquered the world, not in pride, but in humility. He destroyed the devil, not by laughing, but by weeping; he did not scourge, but was scourged; he received a blow but did not give blows. Let us, therefore, imitate our Lord.
Homilies on the Gospel of Saint Mark on Various Topics, Homily 83 (IX)—On Mark 11.15–17 (FOTC 57)

SUFFERING—*Joy*

802. If ever we are sick, if we are beggars, if we are wasting away in sickness, if we are perishing from the cold, if there is no hospitality for us, let us be glad and rejoice; let us receive evil things in our lifetime.
Various Homilies, Homily 86—On the Gospel of Luke 16.19–31 (*The Rich Man and Lazarus*) (FOTC 57)

SUFFERING—*Repentance*

803. Torments, not the disposition of your soul, force you to repent.
Various Homilies, Homily 86—On the Gospel of Luke 16.19–31 (*The Rich Man and Lazarus*) (FOTC 57)

SUFFERING—*Sacrifice*

804. The body in the present world labors more than the soul, for the soul commands, the flesh serves. The toil of the server is one thing, the delights of the commander another. The soul yearns for the Lord. The flesh fasts; it is the body that lies down on the ground in the cold, is imprisoned, scourged in martyrdom, slain, cursed, treated harshly. The soul, too, suffers, but suffering does not reach it except through the body.
Homilies on the Psalms: Second Series, Homily 63, Psalm 83 (84) (FOTC 57)

805. The cross of Christ is the key to Paradise, the cross of Christ opened it. … There is nothing between; the cross and, at once, Paradise. The greatest of pains produces the greatest of rewards.
Various Homilies, Homily 86—On the Gospel of Luke 16.19–31 (*The Rich Man and Lazarus*) (FOTC 57)

The Trinity

THE TRINITY—*Consubstantiality and Unity / God the Father*

806. We believe in the Father, and the Son, and the Holy Spirit, that is true, and that they are a Trinity; nevertheless the kingship is one.
Homilies on the Psalms, Homily 1, Psalm 1 (FOTC 48)

807. With his image, therefore, may he shine upon us, that is, may he shine his image, the Son, upon us in order that he himself may shine upon us, for the light of the Father is the light of the Son.
Homilies on the Psalms, Homily 6, Psalm 66 (67) (FOTC 48)

808. The Son leads to the Father, and the Father leads to the Son; and they are one nature, one substance.
Homilies on the Psalms, Homily 6, Psalm 66 (67) (FOTC 48)

809. In no other, indeed, has the Holy Spirit taken up his abode immediately and perpetually save in the Savior.
Homilies on the Psalms, Homily 7, Psalm 67 (68) (FOTC 48)

810. [Jesus] received from the Father; he received as man; he gives as God; and that which he received, he received for men to give to men. He himself is perfect and is not in need of anything.
Homilies on the Psalms, Homily 7, Psalm 67 (68) (FOTC 48)

811. Every son in truth bears the name of his father.
Homilies on the Psalms, Homily 8, Psalm 74 (75) (FOTC 48)

812. Simply this, the advent of the Son implies the name of the Father.
Homilies on the Psalms, Homily 29, Psalm 102 (103) (FOTC 48)

813. No one is worthy to proclaim the great deeds of the Father except the Son; no one is able to express the might of the Father except him who is himself mighty. He who is himself omnipotent, who is in the bosom of the Father, is able to tell and proclaim the almighty works of Omnipotens.
Homilies on the Psalms, Homily 32, Psalm 105 (106) (FOTC 48)

814. The Father is the beginning, but the Son also is the beginning, for beginning does not have a beginning; if it has another beginning, it has ceased to be the beginning. Whatever, therefore, we attribute to the Father, we attribute also to the Son, for if the Father is in the Son, and the Son in the Father, and all things of the Father are of the Son, and all things of the Son are of the Father, the beginning of the Father is also the beginning of the Son.
Homilies on the Psalms, Homily 36, Psalm 109 (110) (FOTC 48)

815. The Son has always dwelt in the Father, and the Father in the Son.
Homilies on the Psalms: Second Series, Homily 61, Psalm 15 (16) (FOTC 57)

816. The Son was {not} instructed by the Father ... his human nature was instructed by his own divinity. ... It was not a question of the Father giving the Son wisdom and understanding that he did not have before, but of the union of the Father's counsel with the Son's thought.
Homilies on the Psalms: Second Series, Homily 61, Psalm 15 (16) (FOTC 57)

817. Let it be enough for us to know of the Trinity only what the Lord had deigned to reveal.
Homilies on the Psalms: Second Series, Homily 69, Psalm 91 (92) (FOTC 57)

818. This only I know: I am a Christian because I acknowledge one God in Trinity.
Homilies on the Psalms: Second Series, Homily 69, Psalm 91 (92) (FOTC 57)

819. Whether you call him the Father, the Son, or the Holy Spirit, according to the nature of the Trinity which we have expounded in the Gospel, he is both God and Lord.
Homilies on the Psalms: Second Series, Homily 71, Psalm 93 (94) (FOTC 57)

820. Everything that I perceive, I want to understand in Christ, the Holy Spirit, and the Father. Unless I understand in the Trinity that will save me, no understanding can be sweet to me.
Homilies on the Gospel of Saint Mark on Various Topics, Homily 80 (VI)—On Mark 9.1–7 (FOTC 57)

821. Let no one imagine that we are dividing up Christ. That is the accusation of our calumniators, that we make two persons of Christ, one a man and one a God. We believe in the Trinity; we do not believe in a foursome, with two persons in Christ. If Christ, indeed, is two persons, then, by the same token, the Son, who is Christ, is twofold and so there are four persons. We believe in the Father, the

Son, and the Holy Spirit. In regard to the Father and the Spirit, there is no question, for they did not assume a body, something mean or insignificant; but we are now speaking of Christ our God, the Son of God and the Son of man ... Whatever is great refers to the Son of God; whatever slight refers to the Son of man; nevertheless, there is one Son of God.
Homilies on the Gospel of Saint Mark on Various Topics, Homily 81 (VII)—On Mark 11.1–10 (FOTC 57)

822. The Son is God, so that there is no misunderstanding that God is one. By the same process of reasoning through which we affirm the Son to be God, and affirm, moreover, one God in the Father and in the Son, so in the Father and in the Son and in the Holy Spirit there is indeed, a trinity, but one divine nature.
Various Homilies, Homily 87—On the Gospel of John 1.1–14 (FOTC 57)

823. If, then, the Son is the hand and arm of God, and the Holy Spirit is his finger, then there is one substance of the Father and of the Son and of the Holy Spirit. Do not let the inequality of the members cause you to stumble, since the unity of the body builds up.
Commentary on Matthew, Book Two (Matthew 11.2–16.12), 12.28 (FOTC 117)

THE TRINITY—*God the Holy Spirit*

824. O the kindness of the Holy Spirit! He did not say, let them perish, but let them tremble. He wished to point out their fault, not their punishment. They tremble, and the Lord intercedes for them.
Homilies on the Psalms, Homily 26, Psalm 98 (99) (FOTC 48)

825. If the Spirit creates, he is, therefore, God; that is to say, the Spirit creates even as the Father does.
Homilies on the Psalms, Homily 30, Psalm 103 (104) (FOTC 48)

826. Where the Father and the Word of God is, there at once is the Holy Spirit.
Homilies on the Psalms, Homily 57, Psalm 147 (147B) (FOTC 48)

827. Where are the Eunomians, the Arians, the Macedonians who say: 'We do not rank the Holy Spirit with the Father and the Son'? God the Father sends; the Word is sent; but the cure is not complete, except by the breath of the Holy Spirit.
Homilies on the Psalms, Homily 57, Psalm 147 (147B) (FOTC 48)

828. The Paraclete, assuredly, who was to be adored in the assembly of the apostles, is proclaimed equal to the Father and to the Son.
Homilies on the Psalms: Second Series, Homily 66, Psalm 88 (89) (FOTC 57)

829. As I have explained on many occasions, the soul, like the body, has its own limbs and sensory faculties, among which are these [figurative] ears…. We do not need any additional aid in order to come to a knowledge of the Holy Spirit. We obtain him by virtue of a gift, and not a gift of human origin.
Commentary on Galatians, Book One (Galatians 1.1–3.9), 3.2 (FOTC 121)

THE TRINITY—*God the Son*

830. Because we are not able to know him abiding in his Godhead, he assumes our humanity, and in that way we know him.
Homilies on the Psalms, Homily 19, Psalm 89 (90) (FOTC 48)

831. The mystery of the Trinity is also in the baptism of Jesus. Jesus is baptized; the Holy Spirit descends under the appearance of a dove, the Father speaks from heaven.
Homilies on the Gospel of Saint Mark on Various Topics, Homily 75 (I)—On the Beginning of the Gospel of Saint Mark (1.1–12) (FOTC 57)

832. In the presence of the cross, at the very scandal of the Passion, the centurion confesses that {Jesus} is truly the Son of God. Yet in the Church Arius preaches that he is a creature!
Commentary on Matthew, Book Four (Matthew 22.41–28.20), 27.54 (FOTC 117)

833. Our Lord is one and the same Son of God and Son of man. According to both natures, divinity and flesh, he shows signs, now of his greatness, now of his humility. This is why…, though it is a man who was crucified, buried, and shut in the tomb, whom a stone holds back in opposition, nevertheless the things that are done outside show him to be the Son of God: the sun takes flight, darkness falls, the earth quakes, the curtain is torn, the rocks split, the dead are raised, there are services of angels, which even from the beginning of his birth proved that he was God.
Commentary on Matthew, Book Four (Matthew 22.41–28.20), 28.2–3 (FOTC 117)

The Trinity—*Heaven*

834. {Jesus} grew up out of the earth since he was born as man; he has looked down from heaven since God is always in heaven. Assuredly, he is born of earth, but he who was born of earth is always in heaven, for God is everywhere. His appearance on earth was such that he never left heaven.
Homilies on the Psalms, Homily 17, Psalm 84 (85) (FOTC 48)

The Trinity—*Truth*

835. What, in truth, is the foundation, if not the Father and the Son and the Holy Spirit?
Homilies on the Psalms, Homily 18, Psalm 86 (87) (FOTC 48)

Wisdom

WISDOM—*Christ*

836. If wisdom is the tree of life, Wisdom itself, indeed, is Christ.
Homilies on the Psalms, Homily 1, Psalm 1 (FOTC 48)

837. The prophets were in possession of wisdom, but Wisdom itself, as it were, fettered them; they could not fly without Christ.
Homilies on the Psalms, Homily 19, Psalm 89 (90) (FOTC 48)

838. There is no limit to [God's] wisdom; Christ is wisdom. To Wisdom alone, there is no limit.
Homilies on the Psalms, Homily 56, Psalm 146 (147A) (FOTC 48)

WISDOM—*Fearing the Lord*

839. There is no wisdom in those who do not fear the Lord.
Homilies on the Psalms, Homily 37, Psalm 110 (111) (FOTC 48)

WISDOM—*Freedom*

840. Our heart grows blind from the darkness of sins. Foolishness and stupidity are the darkness of our eyes. When, therefore, we have been refreshed in our hunger, and our feet have been released from their fetters, then, with the eye of our heart, we begin to see the light that we had at sometime lost, and we grow in wisdom.
Homilies on the Psalms, Homily 55, Psalm 145 (146) (FOTC 48)

841. One cannot taste of perfect wisdom in an hour, however experienced he may be. One cannot arrive at perfect knowledge without expending a great deal of time in long pursuit of it. First, the dirt is removed; then, the blindness is lifted, and light comes.
Homilies on the Gospel of Saint Mark on Various Topics, Homily 79 (V)—On Mark 8.22–26 (FOTC 57)

WISDOM—*Good Works*

842. Words are of no use whatsoever if knowledge is lacking …. It is of no benefit to you to have facility with words, to have knowledge, if you do not translate them into works.
Homilies on the Gospel of Saint Mark on Various Topics, Homily 81 (VII)—On Mark 11.1–10 (FOTC 57)

843. Indeed, wisdom does not seek the testimony of words but of deeds.
Commentary on Matthew, Book Two (Matthew 11.2–16.12), 11.16–19 (FOTC 117)

844. An idle word is one that is spoken without benefit to both the speaker and the hearer, for example, when we speak about frivolous things to the neglect of serious matters.
Commentary on Matthew, Book Two (Matthew 11.2–16.12), 12.36 (FOTC 117)

WISDOM—*The Mind and Learning*

845. Mere words cannot express adequately what the mind conceives.
Homilies on the Psalms, Homily 1, Psalm 1 (FOTC 48)

846. One preoccupation alone is worthwhile and wholesome—thinking about the Lord.
Homilies on the Psalms, Homily 22, Psalm 93 (94) (FOTC 48)

847. Before we can perform any act or utter any word, our silent reasoning holds it within its own operation and deliberates upon it.
Homilies on the Psalms: Second Series, Homily 61, Psalm 15 (16) (FOTC 57)

848. I have knowledge because I am conscious of my lack of knowledge.
Homilies on the Psalms: Second Series, Homily 69, Psalm 91 (92) (FOTC 57)

849. Is it not better openly to declare ignorance than to rashly assume knowledge from pride?
Homilies on the Psalms: Second Series, Homily 69, Psalm 91 (92) (FOTC 57)

850. Reason is… the ruling faculty of the soul itself.
Various Homilies, Homily 88—On the Nativity of the Lord (FOTC 57)

851. The mind planned to do one thing, the tongue in its zeal slipped ahead.
Various Homilies, Homily 88—On the Nativity of the Lord (FOTC 57)

852. I have not the power to bring forth in words what I conceive in my mind, nor does my tongue give full expression to the joy that is in my heart.
Various Homilies, Homily 93—On Easter Sunday (FOTC 57)

853. It is one thing to confer, quite another to learn. Those who confer are on an equal footing with one another, but the student is always inferior to the teacher.
Commentary on Galatians, Book One (Galatians 1.1–3.9), 2.1–2 (FOTC 121)

854. Christians should not speak for the sake of ostentation, but rather for the sake of edification.

The Apology Against the Books of Rufinus, Book Three, paragraph 3
(FOTC 53)

855. This is the reason why some people remain illiterate literates,
because they refuse to learn what they do not know.
The Apology Against the Books of Rufinus, Book One, paragraph 17
(FOTC 53)

Bibliography

All titles in The Fathers of the Church (FOTC) series are published by the Catholic University of America Press, Washington, D.C.

Jerome. *Commentary on Galatians*. Translated by Andrew Cain. FOTC 121. 2010.

———. *Commentary on Matthew*. Translated by Thomas P. Scheck. FOTC 117. 2008.

———. *Dogmatic and Polemical Works*. Translated by John H. Hritzu. FOTC 53. 1965.

———. *The Homilies of Saint Jerome (Volume I: 1–59, On the Psalms)*. Translated by Sr. Marie Liguori Ewald, IHM. FOTC 48. 1964.

———. *The Homilies of Saint Jerome (Volume II: 60–96)*. Translated by Sr. Marie Liguori Ewald, IHM. FOTC 57. 1966.

———. *On Illustrious Men*. Translated by Thomas P. Halton. FOTC 100. 1999.

Index

NOTE: All numbers in index refer to the number of the saying, not the page number.